LEARN TO KNIT
love TO KNIT

ANNA WILKINSON

PHOTOGRAPHY BY
LAURA EDWARDS

POTTER
CRAFT
New York

CALGARY PUBLIC LIBRARY
NOVEMBER 2013

D1031115

WHEN I WAS LEARNING TO KNIT,

I found the hardest part was getting used to how the yarn and needles felt in my hands and how to manipulate them with my fingers. I remember my hands feeling very rigid and awkward at first, but this feeling quickly passed with just a little persistence, practice, and a few inevitable dropped stitches. Once you have learned the basic knit stitch, and really gotten the hang of it, I believe anything is possible. Every other knitted stitch is just a variation of this one technique and, once you are familiar with the basics, you will be well on your way to mastering any pattern you put your mind to.

The **LEARN TO KNIT** projects in the first section of this book include some very basic and straightforward patterns, so starting with these will enable you to become familiar with the craft and the simpler knit stitches. The patterns then build in difficulty, introducing techniques in different projects, giving you the chance to learn and practice new skills. Some of the **LOVE TO KNIT** projects toward the end of this book may look daunting, but everything is perfectly achievable. Certain projects are simply more time consuming than others and may require more concentration. Just remember, do not panic if you go wrong or drop a stitch. The beauty of knitting is that stitches can easily be unraveled and reknitted.

My career in knitwear really launched for me when I graduated from Winchester School of Art in 2009 and went on to win the Gold Award in the Knitted Textile Awards, which was showcased at the Knitting and Stitching Show at Alexandra Palace. This was an amazing opportunity for me. I met designers, including Debbie Bliss, who I've since had the pleasure of working with on a freelance basis. Before all of this though, a long time ago, I learned to knit at quite a young age. I was taught by my mother, who encouraged me and my two brothers to be creative in all ways; I really wouldn't be writing this book now if it wasn't for all her support. I grew up with color, art, and textiles around me, so now I can't imagine doing anything else. I'm just so grateful to be able to spend my time doing something that I love and call it "work."

While at university, I learned to machine knit; however, for me, there is no comparison between hand knitting and machine knitting. Hand knitting is charming and has personality, plus the labor involved makes it utterly priceless. Whether you wear it yourself or give it as an incredibly generous gift, a hand knit will be loved and worn until it is falling apart and threadbare. You simply cannot create something so special using a machine. The possibilities with hand knitting are endless—you can dream up practically anything and make it yourself. Within this book, I have produced a collection of garments and accessories that I loved designing and making, and each of which I want to wear myself. I really hope that you too enjoy making these projects, whether you are a beginner or have been knitting for years, and I hope that you feel inspired to continue knitting and exploring other patterns and possibilities.

IN YOUR BASIC KNITTING TOOL KIT YOU WILL NEED

KNITTING NEEDLES Knitting needles come in a variety of lengths and thicknesses, depending on the yarn you are knitting with and how many stitches you want to hold on your needle. You will find that when you knit with really thick yarn you will need thicker needles, and the finer the yarn you are using the thinner the needles you will need to use. When you buy yarn, the label always has a suggested needle size on it, but you can always play around with if you want a tighter or looser stitch. You can also get circular needles for knitting in the round. Basically, these are two shorter needles connected by a long nylon wire. You can use circular needles for knitting in rows as well as working in the round, just make sure at the end of each row you swap the needles over in your hands and knit back the way you've just come, rather than continue to knit round and round.

STITCH HOLDERS You will need a few stitch holders when knitting garments. They are used for holding stitches securely that are currently not being worked, for example, around a neckline while you continue with a different section of knitting. These stitches are then later returned to the needles from the stitch holder once you are ready to work with them again. Safety pins are a good alternative for holding a small number of stitches.

CABLE NEEDLES Cable needles are small open-ended needles used for holding just a few stitches at a time and are used when you make the twist in a cable.

YARN NEEDLE Make sure that you have a few blunt-ended yarn needles (called tapestry or darning needles) with a big enough eye to fit yarn through for stitching up knitted garments. It's preferable not to use needles that are too fine or you might find yourself stitching through the knitted yarn and splitting it. A bodkin, which is similar to a needle but is very thick with a big eye, is perfect for stitching up bulky knitted garments.

PINS AND SAFETY PINS These are always useful for pinning seams together before you stitch them, so you know you're sewing evenly.

TAPE MEASURE A tape measure is essential for checking that your gauge is correct. Also, you may find that some patterns use measurements instead of row numbers.

PEN AND PAPER For marking off where you are in your pattern and making other notes.

SCISSORS For snipping yarn.

ROW COUNTERS These are tiny cylinders with rotating numbers that you can slip on one of your knitting needles. Each time you complete a row or round, change the number so you know where you are in your knitting pattern at all times.

NEEDLE GAUGE If you have a collection of vintage knitting needles, which can be picked up from thrift stores or garage sales, a needle gauge is really useful. If the needles are foreign or the number is rubbed off, this will confirm the size.

CROCHET HOOK I love to combine knitting with crochet by adding crocheted buttons or edges to a garment. However, even if you don't want to add crochet to your knits, a crochet hook is essential to a knitter's tool kit for picking up dropped stitches.

CHOOSING YARNS

Select your yarns with care. There are so many amazing hand-knit yarns to choose from, available in a range of different thicknesses and a multitude of colors. I wholeheartedly recommend investing in good-quality yarn as it's more enjoyable to work with and your final knitted piece will look and feel so much nicer to wear and use. Many of the projects in this book are knitted with really stunning yarns (see page 141 for yarn information). However, if you feel the specific recommended yarn is too expensive, another yarn of the same thickness may be substituted. For example, if I recommended a double-knitting-weight yarn, you can substitute this for another similar lightweight yarn. Just make sure that you work a gauge swatch and match the gauge given at the beginning of the pattern. Calculate the amount of a substitute you will need by length rather than by weight.

Whatever you choose, the yarn label will provide information on how to use and care for the yarn. As well as a recommended needle size and gauge, the label will also give the weight and length of the yarn. With the majority of hand-knitted garments, it is best to hand wash gently and leave to dry as flat as possible so the garment does not stretch with the weight of the water as it dries. When buying more than one ball of a specific yarn, check they all have the same dye-lot number. Although the balls of yarn may look the same, there can be subtle color differences between batches, which may show when knitted. While knitting a project, keep a note of the dye-lot number should you need to buy more yarn.

READING PATTERNS

A pattern works through all elements of the project, giving the necessary instructions for every part. Beginning with the size of needles, shade of yarn, and number of stitches cast on, the pattern then continues to outline, row by row, the stitch pattern to follow and indicates when any shaping or other details, such as buttonholes, must be worked. It takes a while to become familiar with the language of knitting patterns, so opposite is a handy list of the most commonly used abbreviations.

When following any pattern, be aware of the different usage of parentheses ( ) and brackets [ ]. Parentheses indicate the different measurements or stitches given for multiple sizes. If you choose to knit the medium size of the Simple Round Neck Sweater on page 53, for example, then you must follow the third size given in the pattern. So where the instructions state, "Using size 3 needles, cast on 111 (115: 121: 127: 133) sts," to knit the medium size, you must cast on 121 stitches, the third number listed. The first size is always shown outside the parentheses and the remaining sizes within them. Likewise, parentheses are used for specific measurements within a pattern of different sizes. So where the instructions state, "Work in stockinette stitch until Back measures 14¾ (14¾: 15¼: 15¼: 15¼)"," to knit the medium size, again, you must follow the third measurement listed which is 15¼". Brackets in knitting patterns have nothing to do with sizing but relate to repeating instructions.

TIPS FOR BEGINNERS

PRACTICE HOLDING THE YARN—Wrap the working end of the yarn (the one attached to the ball) once around the index finger of your right hand. Everyone has their own way of holding the yarn, but while you are learning this is the easiest way to keep the yarn in the correct place. It also helps to produce an even gauge when knitting.

WORK A GAUGE SWATCH—It's so important to get into the habit of knitting a gauge swatch. No matter how tempting it is to dive in and begin the pattern, you need to know that you are working to the correct gauge. If your gauge isn't right, you may end up with a garment that doesn't fit. Use the gauge swatch for practicing your basic stitches. Afterward, put them to use by stitching lots together to make a throw.

READ THE PATTERN—Before you start knitting, take the time to read through all the instructions so you know what to expect. As you work through the pattern, either tick off where you are or keep a row counter handy so you don't get lost or forget which part you've already knitted.

COUNT YOUR STITCHES—Counting your stitches at the end of each row means you'll know immediately when something has gone wrong and can correct the mistake.

START SMALL—As a beginner knitter, start with a small, simple project before increasing the level of difficulty. It's tempting to be brave and try a complex pattern right away, but things could go wrong and leave you feeling frustrated. Practice the basic knit techniques with simple projects, become confident and comfortable with these, before advancing to a more demanding pattern.

JOIN A KNITTING GROUP—Find a knitting buddy or join a group. When teaching yourself to knit, at times it can be frustrating so it's good to be surrounded by others who can answer questions and offer help. You can learn just by watching other knitters. It's also a good way to meet people, share ideas, and feel inspired by what they are creating.

ENJOY YOURSELF—Knitting is a relaxing hobby, so enjoy the craft. Don't get bogged down trying to master instantly every technique and don't panic if you go wrong or drop a stitch. Have fun playing around with the endless possibilities of knitting. Think of ways to use up leftover yarn, make gifts for your friends and express your creativity.

STANDARD ABBREVIATIONS

Knitting patterns use abbreviations for common knitting terms. These are the most widely used abbreviations. Any special abbreviations are included at the start of a pattern, such as the directions for cables.

alt	alternate
beg	begin(ning)
cont	continue(ing)
cm	centimeter(s)
dec	decrease(s)(ing)
DK	double-knitting-weight yarn
foll	follow(s)(ing)
g	gram(s)
inc	increase(s)(ing)
k or K	knit
k2tog	knit next 2 stitches together
kfb	knit into front and back of next stitch
LH	left-hand
m	meter(s)
M1	make one (see page 21)
MC	main color
mm	millimeter(s)
oz	ounce(s)
p or P	purl
p2tog	purl next 2 stitches together
patt(s)	pattern(s)
psso	pass slipped stitch over
p2sso	pass 2 slipped stitches over
rem	remain(s)(ing)
rep	repeat(s)(ing)
rev St st	reverse stockinette stitch
RH	right-hand
RS	right side
skp	slip 1, knit 1, pass slipped stitch over
sl	slip
ssk	slip next 2 sts knitwise, one at a time, insert left-hand needle into fronts of these 2 sts and knit them together
st(s)	stitch(es)
St st	stockinette stitch
tbl	through back loop(s)
tog	together
WS	wrong side
yd	yard(s)
yo	yarn over right needle to make a new stitch
[ ]	work instructions within square brackets as many times as directed

MAKING A SLIP KNOT

"The slip knot is the very first stitch you make when starting any piece of knitting. Without the slip knot you won't be able to work a single row as it acts as the anchor for all knitting, so this is the first technique you need to practice and master. Once you know how, making a slip knot really is so simple."

STEP 1 Make the yarn into a loose figure-eight shape, holding the tail end of the yarn in your right hand and the loop in your left hand.

STEP 2 Pass the yarn from your right hand through the loop in your left hand, ensuring that you keep hold of the tail end of yarn with your right hand and hold the new loop of yarn with your left hand.

STEP 3 Pull this new loop of yarn through the left-hand loop, keeping hold of both the yarn ends in your right hand. This forms a slip knot. Place the slip knot on the knitting needle and pull the ends to tighten. This is the first stitch.

CASTING ON STITCHES

"Casting on is the term used for when you make the first row of stitches on your knitting needle. No matter what you are making, the pattern will always start with the instruction to cast on a certain number of stitches. There are countless different methods for casting on, but this one—called the cable cast-on—is one of the most common and the one that I most often use."

STEP 1 With the slip knot on the left-hand needle—which counts as the first stitch—insert the tip of the right-hand needle up into the stitch from the bottom. The needles should be crossed with the left-hand needle sitting over the right-hand needle.

STEP 2 Holding the needles in your left hand, with your right hand wrap the working end of the yarn—the end attached to the ball—around the back of the right-hand needle then between the needles in a counterclockwise motion.

STEP 3 Catching the working yarn that has just been wound around the needle, bring the tip of the right-hand needle underneath the loop on the left-hand needle and to the front of the stitch.

STEP 4 Pull the new loop farther through. Insert the tip of the left-hand needle up into the loop on the right-hand needle. Slide the right-hand needle out of the loop and pull the working end of the yarn to tighten. This counts as the second stitch.

STEP 5 To make subsequent stitches, insert the right-hand needle between the last two stitches on the left-hand needle and not into the stitch. Wrap the yarn around the right-hand needle, pull the loop through and place on the left-hand needle as before.

WORKING THE KNIT STITCH

"This is the key basic stitch to learn. Most other knitting stitches are a variation on the knit stitch, so this simple four-step process is an important technique to master. In a knitting pattern, the word knit is often abbreviated to a simple 'k.' So 'k1' means 'knit one stitch' while 'k 1 row' means 'knit one row.'"

STEP 1 With the full needle in your left hand and empty needle in your right, insert the tip of the right-hand needle up into the last stitch on the left-hand needle. The needles should be crossed with the left-hand needle sitting over the right-hand needle.

STEP 2 With your right hand, wrap the working end of the yarn around the back of the right-hand needle then through the middle, between the tips of both crossed needles, in a counterclockwise motion.

STEP 3 Catching the working yarn that has just been wound around the needle, bring the tip of the right-hand needle underneath the loop on the left-hand needle. Pull the working yarn through to the front of the stitch.

STEP 4 Slide the stitch just worked off the left-hand needle, leaving the new stitch on the right-hand needle. Repeat these steps until every stitch has been transferred to the right-hand needle. Swap the needles over so the stitches are again in your left hand and continue with the next row.

WORKING THE PURL STITCH

"The next technique to learn is the purl stitch. As perfect partners, the knit and purl stitches are used in combination to create endless stitch patterns. The word purl is often abbreviated in a knitting pattern to 'p.' So 'p1' means 'purl one stitch' while 'p 1 row' means 'purl one row.'"

STEP 1 With the yarn sitting at the front of the work, insert the tip of the right-hand needle up into the last stitch on the left-hand needle. The needles should be crossed with the right-hand needle sitting over the left-hand needle.

STEP 2 With your right hand, wrap the working end of the yarn through the middle, between the tips of both crossed needles, and around the back of the right-hand needle to the front in a counterclockwise motion.

STEP 3 Catching the working yarn that has just been wound around the needle, bring the tip of the right-hand needle underneath the loop on the left-hand needle. Pull the working yarn through to the back of the stitch.

STEP 4 Slide the stitch just worked off the left-hand needle, leaving the new stitch on the right-hand needle. Repeat these steps until every stitch has been transferred to the right-hand needle. Swap the needles over so the stitches are again in your left hand and continue with the next row.

WORKING RIB STITCHES

"Rib patterns are made up of alternate columns of knit and purl stitches. They create a stretchier piece of knitting than either stockinette or garter stitch, which is why ribbing is often used for the waistbands and cuffs of knitted garments."

Different rib patterns are worked using varying combinations of knit and purl stitches; the instructions will specify how many of each stitch to work and in what order. Shown here is single rib, known as k1, p1 rib or 1x1 rib. With ribbing, the movement of the yarn to and from the back and front of the work between stitches is very important. This movement of the yarn is never written into a pattern but it is nonetheless expected.

STEP 1 Knit the first stitch as usual. Bring the yarn toward you to the front of the work, over the top and between the needles. Purl the next stitch as usual. After working this purl stitch, the yarn will naturally be at the front of the work.

STEP 2 Take the yarn to the back of the work, passing it between the needles, ready for the next knit stitch. Repeat these steps—knit one, bring the yarn to the front, purl one, take the yarn to the back—until all the stitches in the row have been worked.

"Knit and purl stitches are the basis of all knitting and once you have learned these two stitches you will be well on your way. By just playing around with where you place these different stitches you can produce an endless number of stitch patterns. Here are just a few examples of what you can do."

TOP LEFT **STOCKINETTE STITCH**—If you knit one row and purl one row alternately you will create stockinette stitch. This stitch has a front side—the knit side—and a reverse side—the purl side. (When the purl side is the front, the stitch is called reverse stockinette stitch.)

TOP RIGHT **GARTER STITCH**—If you knit every row then you will create garter stitch, which looks the same on both sides. You will also create the same look if you purl every row, but as most knitters take longer to work the purl stitch than the knit stitch, to make garter stitch it is quicker to knit every row. This stitch produces a much denser fabric than stockinette stitch.

BOTTOM LEFT **SINGLE RIB STITCH**—single rib is formed by knitting one stitch, purling the next stitch, and repeating this sequence to the end of the row. The columns of knit and purl stitches are maintained in all the subsequent rows. Ribbing can be worked in varying combinations of knit and purl stitches, including k2, p2 and k2, p1.

BOTTOM RIGHT **SEED STITCH**—This is worked in the same way as single rib in that you knit one stitch and then purl the next stitch and continue throughout the row. The difference is if you end a row with a purl stitch when knitting in single rib you start the next row with a knit stitch. When knitting seed stitch, if you finish a row with a purl stitch, you start the next row with a purl stitch, then continue in the p1, k1 pattern to the end of the row.

COMBINATION STITCHES

STOCKINETTE STITCH

GARTER STITCH

SINGLE RIB STITCH

SEED STITCH

BINDING OFF

"Binding off is the term used for finishing a piece of knitting by taking it off the needles. So that the work does not unravel, the stitches must be securely bound off. Whether you knit with a tight or loose tension, keep your stitches looser than you usually would when binding off. This will stop the work from puckering at the bound-off edge. A tight bind-off can look ugly and will spoil your knitting. If you find it hard to keep your bind-off loose, try using a knitting needle slightly bigger than you used in the rest of your knitting (in your right hand) to bind off with."

STEP 1 When binding off knitwise, knit two stitches in the usual way.

STEP 2 Insert the tip of the left-hand needle into the front of the first of these two knitted stitches.

STEP 6 Loosen the final stitch to make a bigger loop and remove the knitting needle.

STEP 7 Pass the cut end of the working yarn through this last loop.

STEP 8 Pull the yarn end to tighten the final loop and secure the last row of your knitted piece.

STEP 3 Carefully lift the first knitted stitch over the second and over the tip of the right-hand needle. Release the stitch you have just lifted over the right-hand needle from the tip of the left-hand needle.

STEP 4 You now have one stitch on the right-hand needle. Knit one more stitch so that you have two stitches on your right-hand needle again, then repeat the move of using the left-hand needle to lift the first stitch on the right-hand needle over the second stitch and off the needle. There should only be either one or two stitches on the right-hand needle at any point while binding off.

STEP 5 When you have been binding off for a full row and have one stitch left on the right-hand needle, cut the working yarn, leaving a fair length so your knitting doesn't unravel.

SHAPING WITH DECREASES

KNIT TWO STITCHES TOGETHER (k2tog)

When shaping a garment you have to decrease and increase the number of stitches on your needles at different points so that you get a shape that fits nicely to the body.

Often in knitting patterns you will find decreases three stitches in from the outside edge. This is called "fully fashioned shaping" and gives a neater result. This technique is very useful if you are working in one color in a simple stitch such as stockinette stitch. However, when working in a stitch pattern, such as a Fair Isle or a lace stitch, it can confuse the pattern repeat if you fully fashion, so you will just as often come across decreases right at the edge of the row.

"The easiest way to decrease the number of stitches in a row, is to knit two stitches together in one new stitch. This is as simple as it sounds. The abbreviation for this is 'k2tog' which just means 'knit 2 together.' As with most things in knitting there are several ways to decrease stitches; this is the most straightforward—and most common—method."

STEP 1 When you are placing the tip of the right-hand needle into the stitches on the left-hand needle, instead of picking up just one stitch pick up the first two stitches at the same time.

STEP 2 Wind the yarn around the needle as you would with a normal knit stitch from back to front.

STEP 3 Catching the yarn that you've just wound around, bring the tip of the right-hand needle through the loops on the left-hand needle.

STEP 4 Then slide the two stitches off the left-hand needle to make one new stitch on the right-hand needle.

KNIT TWO STITCHES TOGETHER THROUGH BACK LOOPS (k2tog tbl)

"This is another really simple way to decrease the number of stitches on your needles. It's very similar to k2tog, however you knit down into the back of the stitches instead of the front. The abbreviation 'k2tog tbl' just means 'knit 2 together through back loops.'"

STEP 1 Instead of knitting up into the two stitches as you would do with a k2tog, place the tip of the right-hand needle down through the two stitches at the back of the work. Push the needle up farther through the two stitches.

STEP 2 Wrap the yarn around the needle as you would with a normal knit stitch, from the back of the work to the front.

STEP 3 Catching the yarn that you've just looped around, pull the tip of the needle through both of the stitches being knitted together.

STEP 4 Slide both stitches off the left-hand needle, leaving just one new stitch on the right-hand needle.

SHAPING WITH INCREASES

KNITTING INTO FRONT AND BACK OF ONE STITCH (kfb)

"When you increase within a row of knitting you can just cast on one stitch at the appropriate point, however this way of increasing gives a far neater finish and is often used in patterns for garments. With this increase method you knit into the front and back of a stitch, making two stitches from one stitch."

STEP 1 Insert the needle into the stitch as usual, wrap the yarn around and pull it through, but do not slip the loop off the needle. Keeping the new stitch on the right-hand needle, knit into the same stitch on the left-hand needle but into the back of the stitch.

STEP 2 Wrap the yarn around the right-hand needle as with any knit stitch, from back to front in a counterclockwise motion.

STEP 3 Catch the yarn that has been wrapped around and bring the tip of the right-hand needle through the stitch.

STEP 4 Slide the old stitch off the left-hand needle. You now have two new stitches on the right-hand needle.

MAKE ONE (M1)

"If, within a knitting pattern, you are asked to increase with the instruction 'M1,' this abbreviation means 'make one stitch.' This method for making the new stitch is the same anywhere in the row."

STEP 1 With the tip of the left-hand needle, lift the horizontal bar between the unworked and worked stitches. If the picked-up loop is too tight to knit easily, loosen it with your fingers.

STEP 2 Knit this new loop from the left-hand needle through the back of the loop—this twists the loop so a hole is not formed under it.

STEP 3 When you count up the stitches at the end of this increase row, you will have one extra stitch.

JOINING IN A NEW BALL OF YARN

"When you come to the end of a ball of yarn, you will have to add a new ball in order to carry on knitting. It is exactly the same procedure as for adding a new color to include a stripe in your knitting. It is best to make a color change at the end of a row, so make sure you leave enough of a tail of the old yarn—at least 4 inches (10cm)—to fasten in the new yarn easily."

STEP 1 Make a cross shape with the new yarn under the old working yarn. Tie the new yarn into a loose knot, with the old yarn lying inside. Slide the new knot up until it touches the knitting needle. Pull both ends of the new yarn to tighten the knot.

STEP 2 Then simply start knitting with the new yarn as usual. When your knitting is complete, you will weave these ends into the wrong side of the knitting.

"Knitting a gauge swatch before you start to knit a pattern is very important, especially if you are a beginner. The point of it is just to ensure that you are knitting in the same gauge that the pattern is written in so you know that your garment will come out the right size and as the designer intended it."

If your gauge matches that given at the beginning of the pattern, then your garment will knit up to the exact size required. Achieving an exact gauge is really important when knitting garments, however, it is less essential for some projects in this book, such at the Striped Scarf on page 32 or the Hand Puff on page 48, because they do not need to fit the body closely.

The gauge given at the beginning of a knitting pattern is almost always written giving the number of stitches in a 4-inch (10cm) square. It's best if you knit at least 1 inch (2.5cm) extra in both directions so that you can take a measurement from the middle of the swatch.

When you have a good-sized swatch knitted up and laid out on a flat surface, take a tape measure and with some pins mark out a 4-inch (10cm) square, then count the stitches within the pins. Each stitch looks like a "V" and you will find generally that you will count more rows (vertically) than stitches (horizontally). This is because knit stitches are usually wider than they are tall. Once you have counted the stitches and the rows within this 4-inch (10cm) square you can compare your gauge to that on the pattern. If it matches, that's great, you can begin to knit the pattern. If it doesn't match, don't worry. If you find that you have more stitches within the 4 inches (10cm) than the pattern states, you knit more tightly than the average knitter and so should try knitting another gauge swatch using slightly thicker needles. If you find that you have fewer stitches within the 4 inches(10cm), then you knit more loosely than the average knitter and so should try knitting another gauge swatch using slightly thinner needles. It may seem a little painstaking to begin with, but it's definitely worth getting right.

SEWING AN INVISIBLE SEAM

MATTRESS STITCH

"Mattress stitch is a method of sewing that gives an almost invisible finish when worked on stockinette stitch, though it can be used on other knit stitches as well. I use it for virtually everything I knit now because I love the way that as you stitch you have the right sides of the knitting facing up, so as you work you are aware of how the knitting will look on the outside."

STEP 1 Lay out the pieces to be joined with right sides face up. Thread a yarn needle with the sewing yarn. Anchor the sewing yarn to both pieces by passing the needle up through the piece on the right and down through the other piece.

STEP 2 In between each stitch, there is a horizontal "bar" that links the two stitches. Insert your yarn needle upward underneath the first two bars in between the columns of stitches at the right side edge.

STEP 3 Insert the needle upward underneath the corresponding two bars on the left side edge. Keep working in this way, alternating between right and left sides, hooking the needle under two bars at a time until all have been stitched.

STEP 4 After you've sewn up a few bars on each side, pull tightly on both ends of the sewing yarn to bring the two sides being sewn together. By tightening the seam, the very edge stitches are turned to the back of the work, leaving a slight ridge.

STEP 5 Once pulled tight, the yarn will effectively disappear as the pieces of knitting are brought together to create a very neat and virtually invisible seam from the outside. Weave in any yarn ends into the ridge on the reverse side of the work.

FIXING DROPPED STITCHES

"If you've dropped a stitch and it has started to 'run,' the most important thing to do is not to panic. It is important to try and fix the dropped stitch as soon as you notice it."

STEP 1 Lay the work flat so you can see the dropped stitch clearly as well as all the strands of the rows above the dropped stitch. If the dropped stitch is within stockinette stitch, it is easier to fix this with the knit side of the work facing.

STEP 2 Insert the crochet hook into the dropped stitch from the front to the back, keeping the dropped strand behind the dropped stitch. Hook the crochet hook onto the strand behind the dropped stitch and pull it through to the front of the dropped stitch.

STEP 3 Keep climbing the ladder of dropped strands by pulling each strand through the dropped stitch until you get back to the row of knitting currently on the needles.

STEP 4 When there are no more dropped strands, put the final dropped stitch onto the left-hand needle and continue to work the row.

UNDOING STITCHES

"If you've realized that you went wrong only a few stitches back, you can easily unravel those stitches and move them from the worked stitches on the right-hand needle, back onto your left-hand needle with the other unworked stitches. You can use this method to undo many rows of knitting— it is slow, but methodical."

STEP 1 If a knit row is facing, hold the working yarn to the back of the work. With the worked stitches in your left hand, insert the right-hand needle from the back to the front into the stitch one row below the last worked stitch on the left-hand needle.

STEP 2 Slide the stitch off the tip of the left-hand needle, keeping the stitch below on the right-hand needle.

STEP 3 Gently pull the working yarn to free the loop of the "below" stitch on the right-hand needle. Continue in this way until you have reached your mistake. When undoing a stitch with a purl row facing, hold the working yarn to the front of the work.

UNRAVELING ROWS

"Every knitter makes a mistake from time to time, and sometimes mistakes go unnoticed even after a few more rows have been worked. This method is the quickest way to unravel—or 'rip out'—the rows to take you back to the good row preceding the mistake."

STEP 1 Thread a needle with colored yarn. Identify the preceding good row of knitting and, with the right side up and working from right to left, pass the needle down through the center "V" of one stitch and then up through the center "V" of the next.

STEP 2 Continue in this way across the row of knitting until all the stitches are caught by the colored yarn. Slide the knitting needle out of all the stitches at the top of the work so that the loops are free and the rows are ready to be unraveled.

STEP 3 Steadily unravel the knitting one row at a time by gently pulling the working yarn until each of the stitches disappear.

STEP 4 Unravel the knitting until you reach the row threaded with colored yarn. This yarn holds all the stitches in the row and stops them from further unraveling. To stop the working yarn becoming tangled, wind all the unraveled yarn back onto the ball.

STEP 5 Thread the stitches back onto the needle from the opposite side to where the working yarn is sitting, so the tip of the needle ends up next to the working yarn. Count the stitches on the needle before removing the safety line of colored yarn.

WORKING A BACK CABLE

"A cable is a twisted column of stitches, whereby the order in which the stitches are knitted is altered by using a short cable needle. Working a back cable creates a right-slanting twist, while working a front cable creates a left-slanting twist. Once you learn how to create a basic twist, you can experiment and knit all sorts of cable patterns."

The following instructions are for "C4B" or "cable four back." This instruction indicates that the width of the whole cable is four stitches wide and that the cable will be twisting over from left to right.

STEP 1 When you reach the row in which the cable twist is worked, work to the column of stitches that is to form the cable.

STEP 2 Slide the correct number of knit stitches (in this case, two stitches) onto the cable needle. The knitting pattern will include instructions on how many stitches are worked within the cable.

STEP 3 Place the cable needle and these two stitches at the back of the work. Knit the next two stitches directly from the left-hand needle.

STEP 4 Slip the first two stitches from the cable needle back onto the left-hand needle.

STEP 5 Knit these two stitches as usual now they are back on the left-hand needle. Continue as the pattern instructs. You will see how the cable twists over from left to right.

WORKING A FRONT CABLE

"Working this front cable is similar to knitting a back cable. However, instead of holding the cable needle at the back of the work, in this case you hold the cable needle at the front of the work."

The following instructions are for "C4F" or "cable four front." This instruction indicates that the width of the whole cable is four stitches wide and that the cable will be twisting over from right to left.

STEP 1 When you reach the row in which the cable twist is worked, work to the column of stitches that is to form the cable.

STEP 2 Slide the correct number of knit stitches (in this case, two stitches) onto the cable needle. Place the cable needle and these two stitches at the front of the work.

STEP 3 Knit the next two stitches directly from the left-hand needle.

STEP 4 Slip the first two stitches back onto the left-hand needle from the cable needle.

STEP 5 Knit these two stitches as usual now they are back on the left hand needle. Continue as the pattern instructs. You will see how the cable twists over from right to left.

learn TO KNIT

STRIPED SCARF
AND MITTENS
WITH GIANT POMPOMS

 *learn*

SIZE
SCARF: One size, 78¾" (200cm) long by 6" (15cm) wide
MITTENS: One size, to fit average size woman's hands

YOU WILL NEED
A 2 x 3½-oz (100g) hanks of a super bulky-weight
 wool yarn (6), such as Quince & Co. Puffin,
 in orange (Apricot)
B 2 x 3½-oz (100g) hanks of a medium-weight wool
 yarn (4), such as Malabrigo Merino Worsted, in mid
 pink (Dusty)—this yarn is used double throughout
Pair each of US sizes 11 and 15 (8mm and 10mm)
 knitting needles
Two 3¼" (8cm) and two 2½" (6cm) cardboard circles

GAUGE
12 stitches and 16 rows to 4" (10cm) square measured
over stockinette stitch using size 15 (10mm) knitting
needles and yarn A single and yarn B double throughout.
However, as the scarf is a simple long knitted strip,
it isn't strictly essential that your gauge matches the
recommended gauge given here. Knitting any scarf is a
really good way to practice your basic knit stitches as
there is no shaping involved and it doesn't have to be an
exact size. As you knit you will become comfortable with
the stitch, and you will have a really lovely accessory once
you are finished. If you decide to make the mittens to go
with your scarf, it is more important to achieve a correct
gauge so that your mittens will fit well and won't either be
too small or resemble an oven mitt.

ABBREVIATIONS
See standard abbreviations on page 9.

**"WHILE KNITTING
THE LONG SCARF,** I simply made up
the stripe pattern as I worked. I varied the
blocks of color by making some stripes very
wide and then interspersed a few narrower
stripes made up of only one or two rows.
You can do the same and just change color
whenever you feel like it. Bear in mind,
however, that if you decide to follow your
own stripe pattern then you may need more
of one color yarn."

TO MAKE THE SCARF

Using A and size 15 (10mm) needles, cast on 18 sts.

ROW I (RS): K to end of row.

ROW 2: P to end of row.

The last 2 rows form the stockinette stitch (St st) pattern, which is worked throughout.

Beg with a k row, cont to work in St st and stripes as foll:

A	34 rows	B	44 rows
B	22 rows	A	14 rows
A	8 rows	B	6 rows
B	4 rows	A	40 rows
A	6 rows	B	4 rows
B	18 rows	A	6 rows
A	12 rows	B	2 rows
B	2 rows	A	4 rows
A	4 rows	B	12 rows
B	2 rows	A	2 rows
A	26 rows	B	4 rows
B	22 rows	A	14 rows
A	6 rows	B	22 rows

Bind off loosely knitwise.

Using two 3¼" (8cm) cardboard circles, make two pompoms (see opposite), one in A to stitch to the pink end of the scarf and one in B to stitch to the orange end of the scarf.

TO MAKE THE LEFT MITTEN

Using A and size 11 (8mm) needles, cast on 24 sts.

ROW I (RS): * K1, p1; rep from * to end of row.

ROW 2: * K1, p1; rep from * to end of row.

The last 2 rows form the single rib (k1, p1 rib) pattern.

Cont to work in single rib as set for 6 rows more.

ROW I (RS): K to end of row.

ROW 2: P to end of row.

The last 2 rows form the stockinette stitch (St st) pattern.

Beg with a k row, cont to work in St st and stripes as foll:

Work 4 rows A and 4 rows B

Cut off A and cont with B only.

SHAPE THUMB

NEXT ROW (RS): K12, turn, cast on 6 sts, p12, turn.

Cont to work on these 12 sts only, leaving rem 6 sts on needle.

Cont to work in St st for 10 rows more.

NEXT ROW (RS): [K2tog] 6 times. *6 sts.*

Cut off yarn, leaving a long tail to stitch up thumb.

Thread yarn end through rem 6 sts, pull up tight, and stitch thumb seam closed.

With RS facing, rejoin B at base of thumb and pick up and k 6 sts across 6 cast-on sts, k to end of row.

P 1 row across all sts.

Beg with a k row, cont to work in St st and stripes as foll:

Work 10 rows B and 10 rows A.

Cut off B and cont with A only.

NEXT ROW: [K2tog] 12 times. *12 sts.*

NEXT ROW: [P2tog] 6 times. *6 sts.*

Cut off yarn, leaving a long tail to stitch up side seam.

Thread yarn end through rem 6 sts, pull up tight, and stitch side seam closed.

To finish, weave in any loose yarn ends.

TO MAKE THE RIGHT MITTEN

Using B and size 11 (8mm) needles, cast on 24 sts.

Work 8 rows in single rib (k1, p1 rib) as given for Left Mitten.

Beg with a k row, cont in St st and stripes as foll:

Work 4 rows B, 2 rows A, and 4 rows B.

SHAPE THUMB

Change to A and with RS facing for next row, cont as foll:

NEXT ROW: K18, turn, cast on 6 sts, p12, turn.

Cont working on these 12 sts only.

Cont to work in St st for 10 rows more.

NEXT ROW (RS): [K2tog] 6 times. *6 sts.*

Cut off yarn, leaving a long tail to stitch up thumb.

Thread yarn end through rem 6 sts, pull up tight, and stitch thumb seam closed.

With RS facing, rejoin A at base of thumb and pick up and k 6 sts across 6 cast-on sts, k to end of row.

P 1 row across all sts.

Beg with a k row, cont in St st and stripes as foll:

Work 4 rows B, 2 rows A, 4 rows B, 2 rows A, and 8 rows B.

Cont with B only.

NEXT ROW (RS): [K2tog] 12 times. *12 sts.*

NEXT ROW: [P2tog] 6 times. *6 sts.*

Cut off yarn, leaving a long tail to stitch up side seam.

Thread yarn end through rem 6 sts, pull up tight, and stitch side seam closed.

To finish, weave in any loose yarn ends.

Using two 2½" (6cm) cardboard circles, make two pompoms (see opposite), one in A to stitch to right mitten and one in B to stitch to left mitten.

MAKING POMPOMS

"Quick and fun to make, a playful pompom can transform an otherwise plain scarf. The more wraps you make around the cardboard ring, the fuller the finished result will be, so it is worth taking a bit more time—and yarn—to create a showstopping pompom."

STEP 1 Cut two circles of cardboard then cut a smaller concentric circle out of the center of both cardboard circles to make a ring.

STEP 2 Holding both cardboard circles together, start wrapping the yarn around the ring. You can thread the yarn onto a blunt-ended yarn needle, which makes this process slightly quicker. As one length of yarn runs out, add in a new length.

STEP 3 Continue wrapping the yarn around the cardboard ring until it is completely covered. The more yarn you wrap around the ring, the fuller the resulting pompom will be.

STEP 4 Make a gap in the wrapped yarn and insert a blade of the scissors so it sits between the two cardboard rings. Keeping the scissors between the two cardboard rings, cut the wrapped yarn taking care not to lose any pieces of yarn from the ring.

STEP 5 Once the wrapped yarn has been cut, slide a length of yarn between the cardboard rings and wrap it tightly around the center of the cut threads. Pull the tie and make a tight knot, leaving a long tail. Ease off the rings. Trim any untidy threads.

SHOPPING BAG
WITH DROPPED-STITCH DETAIL

SIZE
One size

YOU WILL NEED
1 x 17⅝-oz (500g) cone of a super bulky-weight yarn ⓺,
 such as Hooplayarn (a yarn created from the selvages
 of cotton fabric or cotton-mix jersey fabric), in red
 (Bright Red)
US size 17 (12mm) circular knitting needle,
 32" (80cm) long
Size P (12mm) crochet hook
24" (60cm) of strong twill tape (optional)

"THIS SHOPPING BAG IS THE PERFECT PROJECT
to practice working in the round as it doesn't matter if your gauge is a little tight or a little loose because this one-size bag fits all."

GAUGE
Achieving an exact gauge is not essential when knitting this bag, as the finished bag size can vary.

ABBREVIATIONS
See standard abbreviations on page 9.

CASTING ON WITH CIRCULAR NEEDLES

"Always choose the correct length of circular needle to suit the number of stitches being cast on. It is preferable to have a lot of stitches on a shorter wire as you can always bunch the stitches together. Too few stitches on a circular needle and they will become stretched. Before casting on, if the nylon wire of your circular needle appears twisted, dip it in hot water and then pull the wire to straighten."

STEP 1 Cast on the correct number of stitches. Make sure that all the stitches are sitting straight on the needles and wire and check that there are no twists in the line of stitches.

STEP 2 Knit the first stitch on the left-hand point of the needle to join the stitches into a round. Make sure that you pull the first stitch tight to prevent a hole from forming.

TO MAKE THE BAG

Using size 17 (12mm) circular needle, cast on 56 sts (see instructions on page 36 for casting on in the round). Working in the round and making sure you mark the beginning of each round so you know where the next round begins and ends, cont as foll:

ROUNDS 1, 2, AND 3: K to end of round. *

ROUND 4: Wrap yarn around needle 4 times when knitting each stitch to end of round.

NOTE: You will have lots and lots of loops on the wire of the circular needle as you have made 4 loops per knit stitch where ordinarily there would be only one.

ROUND 5: * Slide the first 8 sts off the LH needle and unravel all the loops so that you have eight long stitches, pass the first 4 sts through the loops of the next 4 sts and place them back onto the LH needle, knit these 8 sts as normal, rep from * to end of round.

(See instructions opposite for working this dropped stitch pattern.)

ROUNDS 6, 7, AND 8: K to end of round.

Rep Rounds 4–8 once more.

Rep Rounds 4–8 once more but on Round 4 wrap the yarn around the needle 3 times.

Rep Rounds 4–8 once more but on Round 4 wrap the yarn around the needle 2 times.

SHAPE BASE

ROUND 1: * K3, sl2, k1, p2sso, k2; rep from * to end of round. *42 sts.*

ROUND 2 AND ALL EVEN-NUMBERED ROUNDS: K to end of round.

ROUND 3: * K2, sl2, k1, p2sso, k1; rep from * to end of round. *28 sts.*

ROUND 5: * K1, sl2, k1, p2sso; rep from * to end of round. *14 sts.*

ROUND 7: * K2tog; rep to end of round. *7 sts.*

Cut off yarn, leaving a long tail. Thread yarn end through rem 7 sts, pull up tight, and secure.

Weave in any loose yarn ends into the wrong side of the finished knitting.

TO MAKE THE BAG HANDLES

NOTE: A chain of crochet makes the strongest handles for this type of bag, as they can carry a lot of weight. However, if you prefer not to work the handles in crochet, then use lengths of strong twill tape instead.

TO MAKE CROCHETED HANDLES

Using a size P (12mm) crochet hook, join yarn with a slip stitch to any cast-on stitch on open edge of bag, chain 1, then * work 1 single crochet in each of the next 13 sts, chain 18 *, skip 15 sts; rep from * to * once more, join with a slip stitch to top of first single crochet.

Work 1 round of single crochet on these 62 sts.

Fasten off.

Weave in loose yarn ends.

TO MAKE SEWN HANDLES

Cut two 12" (30cm) lengths of strong twill tape—one for each handle. Pin the ends of each length of twill tape to the inside rim of the open edge of the bag. Stitch in place with reinforced stitching, working a rectangle with a cross inside, at each end of the handle.

"This shopping bag is really quick to knit partly due to the super-bulky yarn it is worked in, which is available in a multitude of colors, but also because of the dropped stitch method used. After knitting so many projects where you must try to avoid dropping stitches, it's very refreshing and fun to work in this technique where holes in your work are a good thing."

WORKING THE DROPPED STITCH

STEP 1 When knitting the dropped stitch, insert the right-hand needle into the first stitch on the left-hand needle, wrap the yarn around the needle the number of times specified—either four, three, or two—instead of the usual once.

STEP 2 Finish knitting the stitch in the usual way by bringing the needle through to the front and sliding the stitch off the left-hand needle.

STEP 3 On the next round, when you reach the dropped stitch, unravel the loops from the left-hand needle to give one long loop.

STEP 4 For this particular pattern, eight dropped stitches are worked in a group and you need to unravel all eight long loops at the same time. Once unraveled, divide the eight long loops into two groups of four.

STEP 5 Pass the first set of four long loops through the center of the second four long loops to form a cross.

STEP 6 Keeping the stitches in this order, slide them back onto the left-hand needle and knit these eight loops in the usual way.

WRISTWARMERS
WITH CONTRASTING RIBBING

SIZE
One size, to fit average size woman's hand

YOU WILL NEED
A fine-weight wool yarn ②, such as Blue Sky Alpaca Melange or Blue Sky Alpaca Sport Weight, in the following colors (amounts given below will make one pair of wristwarmers):

FOR COLORWAY ONE
A   1 x 1¾-oz (50g) hank in orange (Melange, Saffron)
B   1 x 1¾-oz (50g) hank in mustard (Melange, Dijon)

FOR COLORWAY TWO
A   1 x 1¾-oz (50g) hank in mauve (Melange, Bubblegum)
B   1 x 1¾-oz (50g) hank in bright pink (Sport Weight, Hibiscus)

FOR COLORWAY THREE
A   1 x 1¾-oz (50g) hank in pale blue (Sport Weight, Capri)
B   1 x 1¾-oz (50g) hank in pale gray (Sport Weight, Light Gray)

FOR COLORWAY FOUR
A   1 x 1¾-oz (50g) hank in mustard (Melange, Dijon)
B   1 x 1¾-oz (50g) hank in mid blue (Sport Weight, Bluejay)

Pair each of US sizes 3 and 5 (3.25mm and 3.75mm) knitting needles

GAUGE
26 sts and 34 rows to 4" (10cm) square measured over stockinette stitch using size 5 (3.75mm) knitting needles. Adjust needle size as necessary to obtain correct gauge.

ABBREVIATIONS
See standard abbreviations on page 9.

TO MAKE THE WRISTWARMERS (MAKE TWO)
Using size 3 (3.25mm) needles and A, cast on 42 sts.
Change to B.
ROW 1 (RS): * K2, p2; rep from * to last 2 sts, k2.
ROW 2: * P2, k2; rep from * to last 2 sts, p2.
The last 2 rows form the double rib (k2, p2 rib) pattern.
Cont to work in double rib as set for 12 rows more, ending with a WS row.
Change to 5 (3.75mm) needles.
NEXT ROW (RS): K to end of row.
NEXT ROW: P to end of row.
These 2 rows form the stockinette stitch (St st) pattern.
Cont to work in St st until the Wristwarmer measures 8" (20cm) from cast-on edge, ending with a WS row.
Change to 3 (3.25mm) needles and yarn A.
NEXT ROW (RS): K to end of row.
NEXT ROW: * P2, k2; rep from * to last 2 sts, p2.
NEXT ROW: * K2, p2; rep from * to last 2 sts, k2.
Cont to work in double rib as set for 12 rows more.
Bind off loosely in double rib.

TO FINISH
Fold the Wristwarmer in half widthwise, with the wrong sides facing, to form a tube.
Starting from the cast-on edge and working upward, sew together the first 7" (18cm) of the side edges using mattress stitch (see page 24) with B.
Leaving a gap of approximately ¾" (2cm) for the thumbhole, sew together the last 1½" (4cm) of the side edges using mattress stitch with A to match the contrasting color rib.

HIS OR HERS BOBBLE HATS

 *learn*

SIZE
One size, to fit average size man's or woman's head

YOU WILL NEED
A super bulky-weight yarn **6**, such as Blue Sky Alpaca Bulky, in the following colors:

FOR COLORWAY ONE
A   1 x 3½-oz (100g) hank of mustard (Curry)
B   2 x 3½-oz (100g) hanks of bright pink (Azalea)

FOR COLORWAY TWO
A   1 x 3½-oz (100g) hank of cream (Angora)
B   2 x 3½-oz (100g) hanks of mid gray (Gray Wolf)

US size 15 (10mm) circular knitting needle, 16" (40cm) long
Two 3¼" (8cm) cardboard circles

GAUGE
10 stitches and 13 rows to 4" (10cm) square measured over double rib (k2, p2 rib), when fabric is slightly stretched, using size 15 (10mm) knitting needles. Adjust needle size as necessary to obtain correct gauge.

ABBREVIATIONS
s2togkp—slip 2 stitches together, knit 1, pass 2 slipped stitches over.
See also standard abbreviations on page 9.

"TIP: Weaving any loose yarn ends in vertically along the columns of stitches—rather than horizontally across a row of stitches—will help to keep the knitted rib elastic."

TO MAKE THE HAT
Using size 15 (10mm) circular needle and A, cast on 48 sts (see page 36).
Working in the round and marking the beg of each round with a stitch marker or loop of contrasting color yarn, cont as foll:
ROUND 1: * K2, p2; rep from * to end of round.
The last round forms the double rib (k2, p2 rib) pattern.
Cont to work in double rib as set until Hat measures 4" (10cm) from cast-on edge.
Change to B and cont to work in double rib as set until Hat measures 10" (25cm) from cast-on edge.
Divide the stitches on the circular needle into six equal groups, each containing 8 sts. Mark the beg and end of each group with a stitch marker or loop of contrasting color yarn.

SHAPE CROWN
ROUND 1: * K2, p1, s2togkp, p2; rep from * to end of round. *36 sts.*
ROUND 2: * K2, p1, k1, p2; rep from * to end of round.
ROUND 3: * K2, s2togkp, p1; rep from * to end of round. *24 sts.*
ROUND 4: * K2, p2; rep from * to end of round.
ROUND 5: * K1, s2togkp; rep from * to end of round. *12 sts.*
ROUND 6: K to end of round.
ROUND 7: * K2tog; rep from * to end of round. *6 sts.*
Cut off yarn, leaving a long tail. Thread the yarn end through the rem 6 sts, pull up tight, and secure.

TO FINISH
Weave any loose yarn ends into the wrong side of the finished knitting.
Make a pompom in A using 3¼" (8cm) circles of cardboard (see page 35).
Stitch pompom securely to the top of the hat.

"THESE UNISEX BOBBLE HATS are knitted in double rib and simply shaped by working decreases over the last few rounds. The rib creates a stretchy fabric, so this pattern fits a variety of head sizes."

HAND PUFF
AND COLLAR
WITH EMBROIDERY

 *learn*

SIZE
One size

YOU WILL NEED
MC 2 x 3½-oz (100g) balls of a super bulky-weight
bouclé wool yarn (6), such as Rowan Purelife British
Sheeps Breed Bouclé, in mid gray-brown (Light
Brown Masham)

FOR SURFACE EMBROIDERY
A small amount of a lightweight wool yarn (3), such as
Jamieson's DK (a Shetland wool), in each of the
following colors:

A deep red (Cherry)
B turquoise (Splash)
C mid green (Verdigris)
D pale green (Apple)
E gold-green (Bracken)
F bright pink (Fuchsia)

Pair of US size 11 (8mm) knitting needles, for collar
US size 11 (8mm) circular knitting needle, 20" (50cm)
  long, for hand puff
21¾" x 12" (55cm x 30cm) piece of thick cotton batting
21¾" x 13½" (55cm x 34cm) piece of lining fabric in a
  complementary color or print and matching sewing
  thread
2¾-yd (250cm) length and 4" (10cm) length of narrow
  striped grosgrain ribbon, ¼" (6mm) wide
One button, ¾" (2cm) in diameter

GAUGE
10 sts and 16 rows to 4" (10cm) square measured over
seed stitch pattern using size 11 (8mm) knitting needles.
Adjust needle size as necessary to obtain correct gauge.

ABBREVIATIONS
See standard abbreviations on page 9.

"JUST THE THING TO BRIGHTEN
UP A WINTER COAT,
this Hand Puff and Collar duo can be
made in as little as one evening. Worked
in super-bulky yarn, the seed stitch
pattern is quick to work once you get
into the rhythm of knit one stitch, purl
one stitch. I have chosen a bouclé yarn
for a very textured finish and—as this
yarn softens the stitch definition—it
is also quite forgiving if you happen
to make a minor stitch error. Surface
embroidery is a great way to introduce
color into your knitting, without having
to use any special techniques."

TO MAKE THE HAND PUFF

Using size 11 (8mm) circular needle and MC, cast on 50 sts (see page 36).

Working in the round and marking the beg of each round with a stitch marker or loop of contrasting color yarn, cont as foll:

ROUND 1: * K1, p1; rep from * to end of round.
ROUND 2: * P1, k1; rep from * to end of round.

The last 2 rounds form the seed stitch pattern.

Cont to work in seed st as set until Hand Puff measures 11" (28cm) from cast-on edge.

Bind off loosely in seed st.

ADD SURFACE EMBROIDERY

Place the knitted tube in front of you with the open ends at the sides. Using backstitch and the small amounts of contrasting yarn, embroider additional crisscrossing diagonal lines over the surface of the Hand Puff, running from open edge to open edge, to form a "tartan" pattern. You will need to rotate the Hand Puff as you embroider.

TO FINISH

Place the piece of cotton batting inside the knitted tube and, if necessary, trim to fit—the batting should meet end to end without overlapping inside the knitted tube.

Remove the batting from inside the tube and use it to create a template for the lining fabric. Cut the lining fabric to the size of the batting plus an extra ¾" (2cm) all around for the seam allowances.

With right sides together, sew the ends of the lining fabric together to make a tube, taking a ¾" (2cm) seam allowance.

With the lining wrong side out, place the batting on top of the lining fabric tube, then turn back the ¾" (2cm) seam allowance of the lining fabric over the batting and baste the batting and lining together.

Slide the batting and lining inside the knitted tube, then neatly hand-sew the ends of the lining tube to the knitted tube with matching sewing thread.

Pass the 2¾-yd (250cm) length of narrow grosgrain ribbon through the Hand Puff and tie into a bow to create the neck strap. Adjust the length of the ribbon until the Hand Puff is at the perfect height for you.

TO MAKE THE COLLAR

Using a pair of size 11 (8mm) needles and MC, cast on 58 sts.

ROW 1: * K1, p1; rep from * to end of row.
ROW 2: * P1, k1; rep from * to end of row.

The last 2 rows form the seed stitch pattern.

Cont to work in seed st throughout, taking care to keep the stitch pattern correct when decreasing.

ROW 3: Pattern 6, k2tog, pattern 7, k2tog, pattern 7, k2tog, pattern 6, k2tog, pattern 7, k2tog, pattern 7, k2tog, pattern 6. *52 sts.*
ROW 4: Work in seed st to end of row.
ROW 5: Pattern 5, k2tog, pattern 6, k2tog, pattern 6, k2tog, pattern 5, k2tog, pattern 6, k2tog, pattern 6, k2tog, pattern 6. *46 sts.*
ROW 6: Work in seed st to end of row.
ROW 7: Pattern 6, k2tog, pattern 6, k2tog, pattern 6, k2tog, pattern 6, k2tog, pattern 6, k2tog, pattern 6. *41 sts.*
ROWS 8, 9 AND 10: Work in seed st to end of row.

Bind off loosely in seed st.

ADD SURFACE EMBROIDERY

Place the Collar flat in front of you. Using backstitch and the small amounts of contrasting yarn, embroider additional crisscrossing diagonal lines over the surface the Collar, as for the Hand Puff. However, as the Collar is smaller than the Hand Puff, you may prefer to add only one or two lines for a flash of color.

TO FINISH

Fold the 4" (10cm) length of ribbon into a loop and pass the two ends through one top front edge of the Collar and knot at the back to secure.

Sew the button to the opposite front edge to fasten.

SIMPLE ROUND NECK SWEATER
WITH RAGLAN SLEEVES

 learn

SIZE

TO FIT BUST	32"	34"	36"	38"	40"
	81cm	86cm	91cm	97cm	102cm
ACTUAL BUST	36¼"	37¾"	39½"	41¾"	43¼"
	92cm	96cm	100cm	106cm	110cm
LENGTH	23½"	23¾"	22½"	23½"	24"
	59.5cm	60cm	62cm	63cm	63.5cm
SLEEVE SEAM	17"	17"	17"	17½"	17½"
	43cm	43cm	43cm	44cm	44cm

YOU WILL NEED

9 (10: 11: 12: 13) x 1¾-oz (50g) balls of a fine-weight yarn (**2**), such as Frog Tree Alpaca Sport Melange in coral (Coral)
Pair each of US sizes 3 and 5 (3mm and 3.75mm) knitting needles

GAUGE

24 sts and 32 rows to 4" (10cm) square measured over stockinette stitch using size 5 (3.75mm) needles. Adjust needle size as necessary to obtain correct gauge.

ABBREVIATIONS

skp—slip 1 stitch, knit 1 stitch, pass slipped stitch over.
sk2p—slip 1 stitch, knit 2 stitches together, pass slipped stitch over.
See also standard abbreviations on page 9.

TO MAKE THE BACK

Using size 3 (3mm) needles, cast on 111 (115: 121. 127: 133) sts.
ROW 1 (RS): * K1, p1; rep from * to last st, k1.
ROW 2 (WS): * P1, k1; rep from * to last st, p1.
The last 2 rows form the single rib (k1, p1 rib) pattern.
Cont to work in single rib as set until Back measures 1½" (4cm) from cast-on edge, ending with a WS row.
Change to size 5 (3.75mm) needles.
Beg with a k row, work in St st until Back measures 14¾ (14¾: 15¼: 15¼: 15¼)"/37.5 (37.5: 38.5: 38.5: 38.5)cm from cast-on edge, ending with a WS row.

SHAPE RAGLANS
Bind off 5 sts at beg of next 2 rows. *101 (105: 111: 117: 123) sts.*
Work even in St st for 2 rows.
ROW 1: K3, skp, k to last 5 sts, k2tog, k3.
ROW 2: P to end of row.
The last 2 rows set the position of decs for raglan shaping.
[Rep Rows 1 and 2] 3 times, working decs as set. *93 (97: 103: 109: 115) sts.*
Work even in St st for 2 rows.
[Rep Rows 1 and 2] 4 times, working decs as set. *85 (89: 95: 101: 107) sts.*
Work even in St st for 2 rows.
[Rep Rows 1 and 2] 3 times, working decs as set. *79 (83: 89: 95: 101) sts.*
Work even in St st for 2 rows.
[Rep Rows 1 and 2] 5 times, working decs as set. *69 (73: 79: 85: 91) sts.*

"TIP: For a neat, even neck band, it easier to pick up fewer stitches over a smaller area, so divide up the neck edge into sections. For example, rather than trying to pick up 16 sts evenly along the left front neck in one go, break it down into four sets of four stitches.**"**

ROW 3: K3, sk2p, k to last 6 sts, k3tog, k3.
ROW 4: P to end of row.
65 (69: 75: 81: 87) sts. **
Rep Rows 3 and 4 once more.
Rep Rows 1 and 2 once.
[Rep Rows 3 and 4] 3 (3: 3: 3: 4) times.
[Rep Rows 1 and 2] 1 (1: 2: 3: 3) times.
[Rep Rows 3 and 4] 2 (3: 3: 4: 4) times.
Rep Row 1 once.
NEXT ROW (WS): P3, p2tog, p to last 5 sts, p2tog tbl, p3.
Rep Row 1 once.
NEXT ROW (WS): P3, p2tog, p to last 5 sts, p2tog tbl, p3.
Bind off rem 29 (29: 33: 33: 35) sts.

TO MAKE THE FRONT

Work as given for Back to **. *65 (69: 75: 81: 87) sts.*

SHAPE NECK
NEXT ROW (RS): K3, sk2p, k until there are 23 (25: 28: 31: 34) sts on RH needle, turn, leave rem unworked sts on a stitch holder.
Work each side of next separately.
Work left side of neck on these 23 (25: 28: 31: 34) sts only as foll:
NEXT ROW (WS): Bind off 2 sts at neck edge, p to end of row. *21 (23: 26: 29: 32) sts.*
ROW I: K3, skp, k to end of row.
ROW 2: P2tog, p to end of row. *19 (21: 24: 27: 30) sts.*
ROW 3: K3, sk2p, knit to end.
ROW 4: P2tog, p to end of row.
Rep Rows 3 and 4 once more. *13 (15: 18: 21: 24) sts.*

FOR 5TH SIZE ONLY
Rep Rows 3 and 4 once more. *21 sts.*

FOR 1ST AND 2ND SIZES ONLY
ROW I: K3, skp, k to end of row.
ROW 2: P to end of row. *11 (13: –: –: –) sts.*

FOR 3RD SIZE ONLY
ROW I: K3, skp, k to end of row.
ROW 2: P2tog, p to end of row.
ROW 3: K3, skp, k to end of row.
ROW 4: P to end of row. *– (–: 13: –: –) sts.*

FOR 4TH AND 5TH SIZES ONLY
ROW I: K3, skp, k to end of row.
ROW 2: P to end of row.
ROW 3: K3, skp, k to end of row.
ROW 4: P to end of row. *– (–: –: 17: 17) sts.*

FOR 1ST, 2ND, 4TH, AND 5TH SIZES ONLY
ROW I: K3, skp, k to end of row.
ROW 2: P2tog, p to end. *9 (11: –: 15: 15) sts.*

FOR ALL SIZES
ROW 3: K3, sk2p, k to end of row.
ROW 4: P to end of row.
Rep the last 2 rows until 5 sts rem.
NEXT ROW (RS): K3, skp.
NEXT ROW: P2tog, p2.
NEXT ROW: K1, skp.
NEXT ROW: P2tog.
Fasten off.
With RS of work facing and using size 5 (3.75mm) needles, rejoin yarn to rem sts from stitch holder.
NEXT ROW: Bind off 15 sts, k to last 6 sts, k3tog, k3.
Work right side of neck to match left side of neck, reversing all shaping.
NOTE: Remember to work k2tog instead of skp for raglan decs worked on a RS row, work k3tog instead of sk2p for raglan double decs worked on a RS row and work p2tog tbl instead of p2tog for raglan decs worked on a WS row.

TO MAKE THE SLEEVES (MAKE TWO)

Using size 3 (3mm) needles, cast on 51 (51: 53: 53: 55) sts.
ROW I: * K1, p1; rep from * to last st, k1.
ROW 2: * P1, k1; rep from * to last st, p1.
The last 2 rows form the single rib (k1, p1 rib) pattern.
Cont to work in single rib as set until Sleeve measures 1½" (4cm) from the cast-on edge, ending with a WS row.
Change to size 5 (3.75mm) needles.
ROW I (RS): K1, M1, k to last st, M1, k1.
ROWS 2, 4, 6, AND 8: P to end of row.
ROWS 3, 5, AND 7: K to end of row.
The last 8 rows set the position of incs for sleeve shaping.
Rep the last 8 rows until there are 81 (81: 83: 83: 85) sts.
Work even in St st until Sleeve measures 17 (17: 17: 17½: 17½)"/43 (43: 43: 44: 44)cm from cast-on edge, ending with a WS row.

SHAPE RAGLANS
Bind off 5 sts at beg of next 2 rows. *71 (71: 73: 73: 75) sts.*
ROWS I AND 3: K3, skp, k to last 5 sts, k2tog, k3.
ROWS 2 AND 4: P to end of row.
ROW 5: K3, sk2p, k to last 6 sts, k3tog, k3.
ROW 6: P to end of row.
[Rep Rows 1–6] 4 times more.
[Rep Rows 1 and 2] 4 times.

Rep Row 1 once more.
Work even in St st for 3 rows. *21 (21: 23: 23: 25) sts.*
[Rep Rows 1 and 2] 1 (1: 1: 1: 2) times.

FOR 2ND, 4TH, AND 5TH SIZES ONLY
Work even in St st for 2 rows.

FOR ALL SIZES
Rep Row 1 once.
Work even in St st for 3 rows.
Rep the last 4 rows 3 (3: 4: 4: 4) times more.

FOR 4TH AND 5TH SIZES ONLY
Work even in St st for 2 rows.

FOR ALL SIZES
NEXT ROW (RS): K3, skp, k1, k2tog, k3.
NEXT ROW: P to end of row.
Bind off rem 9 sts.

TO FINISH
Weave in any loose yarn ends.
Sew each Front shaped raglan edge to a shaped raglan edge of a Sleeve.
Sew the Back right shaped raglan edge to the left shaped raglan edge of a Sleeve.
Leave the Back left raglan edge open.

WORK NECK BAND
With RS facing and using size 3 (3mm) needles, pick up and k 9 sts along top of left sleeve, 16 sts down left side of front neck, 15 sts along center front neck, 16 sts up right side of front neck, 9 sts along top of right sleeve, and 29 (29: 33: 33: 35) sts along back neck. *94 (94: 98: 98: 100) sts.*
Work 6 rows in single rib.
Bind off loosely in rib.

TO FINISH
Sew Back left shaped raglan edge to right shaped raglan edge of a Sleeve and sew together the ends of the neck band.
Sew side and sleeve seams using mattress stitch.

PICKING UP STITCHES FOR A NECK BAND

"It is possible to knit a neck band separately and then sew it in place, but I prefer to pick up stitches around the neck edge and knit on the neck band. This can be done using either straight needles or a circular needle."

Hold the working yarn at the back of the knitting. From the front of the work, insert the tip of the needle into the space between the edge stitch and next stitch. Wrap the working yarn around the needle, then bring the needle and yarn through to the right side of the work. Continue in this way until the required number of stitches have been picked up.

CROPPED CARDIGAN
WITH CABLED SLEEVES

SIZE

TO FIT BUST	32"	34"	36"	38"
	81cm	86cm	91cm	97cm
ACTUAL BUST	34¼"	36½"	38½"	40¾"
	87cm	92.5cm	98cm	103.5 cm
LENGTH OF	16¾"	16¾"	17½"	18"
SHORT VERSION	42.5cm	42.5cm	44.5cm	45.5cm
LENGTH OF	19½"	19½"	20¼"	20¾"
LONG VERSION	49.5cm	49.5cm	51.5cm	52.5
SLEEVE SEAM	15"	15"	15½"	15½"
	37cm	37cm	38cm	38cm

YOU WILL NEED

A lightweight (a double-knitting-weight) yarn (3), such as
   Juno Fibre Arts Juno Pearl in the following colors:

FOR THE SHORT VERSION
4 (5: 6: 7) x 3½-oz (100g) hanks in gold (Goldmine)

FOR THE LONG VERSION
4 (5: 6: 7) x 3½-oz (100g) hanks in pale green
   (Fresh Greens)

Pair each of US sizes 3 and 6 (3.25mm and 4mm)
   knitting needles
Cable needle
6 buttons (for short version)or 8 buttons (for long version)

GAUGE

22 sts and 30 rows to 4" (10cm) square measured over
stockinette stitch using size 6 (4mm) needles. Adjust
needle size as necessary to obtain correct gauge.

ABBREVIATIONS

BC back cross—slip 1 stitch onto cable needle, hold
at back of work, knit 2 stitches, purl 1 stitch from
cable needle.
FC front cross—slip 2 stitches onto cable needle,
hold at front of work, purl 1 stitch, knit 2 stitches from
cable needle.
LT left twist—with RH needle behind LH needle, skip
first stitch and knit into back loop of second stitch, insert
RH needle into backs of both stitches, knit 2 together
through back loops.
MK make knot—(k1, p1, k1, p1, k1, p1, k1) into next
stitch, pass 2nd, 3rd, 4th, 5th, 6th, and 7th sts on RH
needle separately over last stitch made.
RT right twist—knit 2 together leaving stitches on
LH needle, then inserting RH needle from front between
2 stitches of k2tog, knit first stitch again, slip both stitches
together from LH needle.
See also standard abbreviations on page 9.

BRIAR ROSE PATTERN USED ON BACK AND FRONT (A 12-ROW REPEAT WORKED OVER 13 STS)

ROW I (WS): K3, p1, k1, p2, k2, p1, k3.
ROW 2: P3, LT, p1, LT, RT, p3.
ROW 3: K4, p2, k2, p1, k4.
ROW 4: P2, (k1, yo, k1) into next st, turn, p3, turn, k3 wrapping yarn twice around needle for each st, p1, LT, p1, RT, p4.
ROW 5: K4, p2, k1, p1, k2, sl next 3 sts dropping extra wraps, sl same 3 sts back onto LH needle, p3tog tbl, k2.
ROW 6: P2, LT, p1, k1 tbl, RT, LT, p3.
ROW 7: K3, p1, k2, p2, k1, p1, k3.
ROW 8: P3, LT, RT, p1, RT, p3.
ROW 9: K4, p1, k2, p2, k4.
ROW 10: P4, LT, p1, RT, p1, (k1, yo, k1) into next st, turn, p3, turn, k3 wrapping yarn twice around needle for each st, p2.
ROW II: K2, sl next 3 sts dropping extra wraps, sl same 3 sts back onto LH needle, p3tog, k2, p1, k1, p2, k4.
ROW I2: P3, RT, LT, k1 tbl, p1, RT, p2.
Repeat Rows 1–12 to from the pattern.

TO MAKE THE BACK

Using size 3 (3.25mm needles), cast on 96 (102: 108: 114) sts.

FOR 1ST AND 3RD SIZES ONLY
ROW I (RS): * K2, p2; rep from * to end of row.
ROW 2: * K2, p2; rep from * to end of row.

FOR 2ND AND 4TH SIZES ONLY
ROW I (RS): * K2, p2; rep from * to last 2 sts, k2.
ROW 2: *P2, k2; rep from * to last 2 sts, p2.

ALL SIZES
The last 2 rows form the double rib (k2, p2 rib) pattern. Cont to work in double rib as set for 20 rows more. Change to size 6 (4mm) needles.
Beg with a k row, work in St st until Back measures 6 (6: 6¼: 6¾)"/15 (15: 16: 17)cm for the short version or 8¾ (8¾: 9: 9½)"/22 (22: 23: 24)cm for the long version from cast-on edge, ending with a WS row.

SHAPE RAGLAN AND PLACE BRIAR ROSE PATTERN
NEXT ROW (RS): Bind off 4 sts knitwise, k to end of row.
NEXT ROW (WS): Bind off 4 sts purlwise (st on RH needle after bind-off becomes selvage st), work Row 1 of Briar Rose pattern over 13 sts, p to last 14 sts, work Row 1 of Briar Rose pattern over 13 sts, p1.
NOTE: The selvage stitch is always a knit stitch on RS rows and a purl stitch on WS rows.

Cont to work Briar Rose pattern on first and last 14 sts of each row but AT THE SAME TIME work raglan shaping by dec on 15th and 16th sts from beg and end of each row on next and every foll 4th row until 58 (70: 76: 88) sts rem, working dec row as foll:
NEXT ROW (RS): K1, work Briar Rose pattern over next 13 sts, skp, k to 16th st from end of row, k2tog, work Briar Rose pattern over next 13 sts, k1.
NOTE: The dec row is always a RS row and the decs are made just inside the Briar Rose pattern.
NEXT ROW (WS): P1, work Briar Rose pattern over next 13 sts, p to last 14 sts, work Briar Rose pattern over next 13 sts, p1.
Keeping Briar Rose pattern correct, work decs as set on next and every foll alt row until 36 (36: 38: 38) sts rem.
NEXT ROW (WS): P1, work Briar Rose pattern over next 13 sts, p to last 14 sts, work Briar Rose pattern over next 13 sts, p1.
Place rem sts on a stitch holder.

TO MAKE THE LEFT FRONT

With size 3 (3.25mm) needles, cast on 47 (50: 53: 56) sts.

FOR 1ST SIZE ONLY
ROW I: P1, * k2, p2; rep from * to last 2 sts, k2.
ROW 2: * P2, k2; rep from * to last 3 sts, p2, k1.

FOR 2ND SIZE ONLY
ROW I: * K2, p2; rep from * to last 2 sts, k2.
ROW 2: * P2, k2; rep from * to last 2 sts, p2.

FOR 3RD SIZE ONLY
ROW I: K1, * p2, k2; rep from * to end of row.
ROW 2: * P2, k2; rep from * to last st, p1.

FOR 4TH SIZE ONLY
ROW I: * P2, k2; rep from * to end of row.
ROW 2: * P2, k2; rep from * to end of row.

ALL SIZES
The last 2 rows form the double rib (k2, p2 rib) pattern. Cont to work in double rib as set for 20 rows more. Change to size 6 (4mm) needles.
Beg with a k row, work in St st until Left Front measures 6 (6: 6¼: 6¾)"/15 (15: 16: 17)cm for the short version or 8¾ (8¾: 9: 9½)"/22 (22: 23: 24)cm for the long version from cast-on edge and matches Back to raglan, ending with a WS row.

SHAPE RAGLAN AND PLACE BRIAR ROSE PATTERN
NEXT ROW (RS): Bind off 4 sts knitwise, k to end of row.

NEXT ROW (WS): P to last 14 sts, work Row 1 of Briar Rose pattern over next 13 sts, p1.

NOTE: The selvage stitch is always a knit stitch on RS rows and a purl stitch on WS rows.

Cont to work the Briar Rose pattern as set but AT THE SAME TIME work raglan shaping by dec on 15th and 16th sts on next and every foll 4th row until 28 (34: 37: 43) sts rem, working dec row as foll:

NEXT ROW (RS): K1, work Briar Rose pattern over next 13 sts, skp, k to end of row.

NOTE: The dec row is always a RS row and the decs are made just inside the Briar Rose pattern.

NEXT ROW (WS): P1, work Briar Rose pattern over next 13 sts, p to end of row.

Keeping Briar Rose pattern correct, work decs as set on next and every foll alt row until 25 (25: 28: 28) sts rem.

SHAPE NECK

NEXT ROW (WS): Bind off 7 (7: 8: 8) sts purlwise, p to end last 14 sts, work Briar Rose pattern over next 13 sts, p1.

Keeping Briar Rose pattern correct, dec 1 st at neck edge as set on next 8 rows but AT THE SAME TIME dec 1 st at raglan edge on next and every alt row until 6 (6: 8: 8) sts rem.

Keeping Briar Rose pattern correct, dec 1 st at raglan edge on next and 2 (2: 4: 4) foll alt RS rows until 3 sts rem.

NEXT ROW (WS): Work 1 row in pattern.

NEXT ROW (RS): K1, skp.

NEXT ROW (WS): P to end of row.

NEXT ROW (RS): Skp.

Fasten off.

TO MAKE THE RIGHT FRONT

Work as given for Left Front, reversing all shaping and working k2tog instead of skp for decs at raglan shaping.

HOLLOW OAK PATTERN USED ON SLEEVES (A 20-ROW REPEAT WORKED OVER 15 STS)

ROWS 1, 3, 5, AND 7 (WS): K5, p5, k5.
ROW 2: P5, k2, MK, k2, p5.
ROW 4: P5, MK, k3, MK, p5.
ROW 6: Rep row 2.
ROW 8: P4, BC, p1, FC, p4.
ROW 9: K4, p2, k1, p1, k1, p2, k4.
ROW 10: P3, BC, k1, p1, k1, FC, p3.
ROW 11: K3, p3, k1, p1, k1, p3, k3.
ROW 12: P2, BC, [p1, k1] twice, p1, FC, p2.
ROW 13: K2, p2, [k1, p1] 3 times, k1, p2, k2.
ROW 14: P2, k3, [p1, k1] twice, p1, k3, p2.

ROWS 15: Rep row 13.
ROW 16: P2, FC, [p1, k1] twice, p1, BC, p2.
ROW 17: Rep row 11.
ROW 18: P3, FC, k1, p1, k1, BC, p3.
ROW 19: Rep row 9.
ROW 20: P4, FC, p1, BC, p4.
Repeat Rows 1–20 to form the pattern.

TO MAKE THE SLEEVES (MAKE TWO)

With size 3 (3.25mm) needles, cast on 43 (43: 45: 45) sts.

ROW 1: K1, * p2, k2; rep from * to end of row.
ROW 2: * P2, k2; rep from * to last st, p1.

The last 2 rows form the double rib (k2, p2 rib) pattern.

Cont to work in double rib as set for 12 rows more.

Change to size 6 (4mm) needles.

Beg with a p row, work in St st with Hollow Oak pattern over center 15 sts but AT THE SAME TIME inc 1 st at both ends of first and every foll 4th row until 91 (91: 95: 95) sts.

Keeping St st and Hollow Oak pattern correct, work even for 6 rows, ending with a p row.

SHAPE RAGLANS

Keeping St st and Hollow Oak pattern correct, bind off 4 sts at beg of next 2 rows.

NEXT ROW (RS): K3, skp, work to last 5 sts, k2tog, k3.

Keeping St st and Hollow Oak pattern correct, dec at raglans as set on every foll 4th row until 71 (71: 75: 75) sts rem, ending with a WS row.

Keeping St st and Hollow Oak pattern correct, cont to work decs at raglan edges as set on next and every foll alt row until 13 sts rem, ending with a WS row.

Place rem sts on a stitch holder.

NOTE: When Sleeve becomes narrow and there is no more St st, maintain raglan shaping by working decs in Hollow Oak pattern. The first and last 5 sts of each row are worked in pattern as set on RS rows and purled on WS rows.

YOU WILL HAVE COMPLETED:

1ST AND 2ND SIZES ONLY
9 complete Hollow Oak pattern repeats, plus 1 extra row.

3RD AND 4TH SIZES ONLY
9 complete Hollow Oak pattern repeats, plus 9 extra rows.

TO FINISH

Sew the raglan edges of the Left and Right Fronts and Back to the raglan edges of the Sleeves.

WORK NECK BAND

With RS facing and using size 3 (3.25mm) needles, beg at Right Front, pick up and k 20 (20: 23: 23) sts along right side of neck, k 13 sts from top of right sleeve, k 36 (36: 38: 38) sts from Back neck, 13 sts from top of left sleeve, then pick up and k 20 (20: 23: 23) sts down left side of neck. *102 (102: 110: 110) sts.*

ROW 1 (RS): * K2, p2; rep from * to last 2 sts, k2.

ROW 2: *P2, k2; rep from * to last 2 sts, p2.

The last 2 rows form the double rib (k2, p2 rib) pattern. Cont to work in double rib as set until neck band measures 1¼" (3cm).

Bind off evenly in rib.

Sew side and sleeve seams using mattress stitch.

WORK BUTTON BAND

Using size 3 (3.25mm) needles, cast on 10 sts. Work in double rib as given for Neck Band until button band stretches up Left Front to top of neck band. Bind off evenly in rib.

Slip stitch button band in place.

Mark position of 6 buttons for short version and 8 buttons for long version on Left Front button band. The first buttonhole must sit in the center of the neck band and the last button must sit ½" (1cm) above bottom edge; evenly space remaining buttons between these two.

BUTTONHOLE BAND

Work as given for button band but AT THE SAME TIME work buttonholes to correspond with marked positions on the button band (see instructions below)

Sew buttons securely to button band to correspond with buttonholes.

"This versatile method of making buttonholes can be adapted according to the size of buttons you are using. Simply bind off more or fewer stitches to adjust the size of the buttonhole."

MAKING A BUTTONHOLE

STEP 1 On the first buttonhole row, work as usual to the buttonhole position. Work two stitches, then lift the first stitch over the second stitch to bind off one stitch. Repeat this until 4 stitches have been bound off.

STEP 2 Work to the end of the first buttonhole row as usual. On the next row, work to the position of the bound-off stitches on the previous row and then turn the work.

STEP 3 Using the cable cast-on method (see page 11), cast on 4 stitches. Before placing the last cast-on stitch onto the left-hand needle, bring the yarn forward to the front. Turn and complete the row as usual.

LACE COLLAR
WITH TIE FASTENING

 *learn*

SIZE
One size (adjustable)

YOU WILL NEED
MC A lace-weight yarn (0), such as Buffalo Gold
Lux Lace or Natural Dye Studio Angel 2-ply Lace
A A lace-weight yarn (0), such as Fyberspates
Scrumptious Lace or Habu Non-Twist Cotton
Bouclé Lace

FOR COLORWAY ONE
MC 1 x 1⅜-oz (40g) hank in dark green (Lux Lace, Pine)
A small amount in gold (Scrumptious Lace, Gold)

FOR COLORWAY TWO
MC 1 x 3½-oz (100g) hank in pink (Angel 2-ply Lace,
Bobby's Girl)
A small amount in pale green (Non-Twist Cotton
Bouclé Lace, Aqua)

Pair each of US sizes 3 and 4 (3mm and 3.5mm)
knitting needles
One self-cover button, 1" (2.5cm) in diameter (optional)

GAUGE
The 12-stitch lace pattern repeat measures approximately
2¼" (6cm) using size 3 (3mm) needles. However, do not
worry too much if your gauge is not completely accurate
as the collar is adjustable.

ABBREVIATIONS
See standard abbreviations on page 9.

TO MAKE THE LEFT SIDE OF COLLAR
Wind a length of yarn A into a small bobbin (see page 90).
Using size 3 (3mm) needles and A, cast on 61 sts using the
lace cast-on method.
NOTE: For the lace cast-on method, work as on page 11
but pass the RH needle through the loop on the LH needle
to form the new stitch, rather than between the loops.
K 3 rows.
Keeping 3 knit sts in A at each edge and twisting A and
MC around each other when changing colors to avoid a
hole, work 12-row repeat lace pattern as foll:
ROW 1 (RS): K3 in A, change to MC, k1, [k2tog, yo, k1, yo,
k2tog tbl, k7] 4 times, k2tog, yo, k1, yo, k2tog tbl, k1, join
in bobbin of A, k3 in A.
ROW 2 AND ALL EVEN-NUMBERED ROWS: K3 in A,
change to MC, p to last 3 sts, k3 in A.
ROW 3: K3 in A, change to MC, k2tog, [yo, k3, yo, k2tog
tbl, k5, k2tog] 4 times, yo, k3, yo, k2tog tbl, k3 in A.
ROW 5: Rep row 1.
ROW 7: K3 in A, change to MC, k1, [k6, k2tog, yo, k1, yo,
k2tog tbl, k1] 4 times, k6, k3 in A.
ROW 9: K3 in A, change to MC, k1, [k5, k2tog, yo, k3, yo,
k2tog tbl] 4 times, k6, k3 in A.
ROW 11: Rep row 7.
ROW 12: Rep row 2.
The last 12 rows from the lace pattern.
Change to size 4 (3.5mm) needles and work 12-row repeat
lace pattern but AT THE SAME TIME work decs on front
and back center edges as foll:
ROW 1: K3 in A, change to MC, k1, [k2tog, yo, k1, yo, k2tog
tbl, k7] 4 times, k2tog, yo, k1, yo, k2tog tbl, k1, k3 in A.
ROW 2 AND ALL EVEN-NUMBERED ROWS: K3 in A,
change to MC, p to last 3 sts, k3 in A.
ROW 3: K3 in A, change to MC, k2tog, k3, yo, k2tog tbl,
k5, k2tog, [yo, k3, yo, k2tog tbl, k5, k2tog] 3 times, yo,
k3, yo, k2tog tbl, k3 in A. *60 sts.*

WORKING SIMPLE LACE STITCHES

"Lace knitting is made up of a series of increases and decreases to create openwork patterns, in which the working yarn is taken over the right-hand needle to make a yarn over to form a decorative hole. There are various methods for working yarn overs, but this is the simplest. It is used when you have just worked a knit stitch or a knit two together decrease and are continuing with another knit stitch after the yarn over."

STEP I Following the lace pattern, work to the position of the decrease.

STEP 2 Work the decrease by knitting two stitches together as given in the instructions.

STEP 3 Begin the yarn over by bringing the working yarn to the front of the work between the tips of the two needles.

STEP 4 Take the yarn to the back of the work over the right-hand needle to complete the yarn over and knit the next stitch as usual.

ROW 5: K3 in A, change to MC, k2tog, k1, yo, k2tog tbl, k7, [k2tog, yo, k1, yo, k2tog tbl, k7] 3 times, k2tog, yo, k1, yo, k2tog tbl, k1, k3 in A. *59 sts.*

ROW 7: K3 in A, change to MC, k2tog, k3, k2tog, yo, k1, yo, k2tog tbl, k1, [k6, k2tog, yo, k1, yo, k2tog tbl, k1] 3 times, k4, k2tog, k3 in A. *57 sts.*

ROW 9: K3 in A, change to MC, k2tog, k1, k2tog, yo, k3, yo, k2tog tbl, [k5, k2tog, yo, k3, yo, k2tog tbl] 3 times, k5, k3 in A. *56 sts.*

ROW II: K3 in A, change to MC, k2tog, k1, k2tog, yo, k1, yo, k2tog tbl, k1, [k6, k2tog, yo, k1, yo, k2tog tbl, k1] 3 times, k3, k2tog, k3 in A. *54 sts.*

Cut off MC and cont in A only.
Change to size 3 (3mm) needles.

ROW I: K3, k2tog, k to end of row. *53 sts.*

ROW 2: K to end of row.

ROW 3: K3, k2tog, k to last 5 sts, k2tog, k3. *51 sts.*

WORK PICOT BIND-OFF

NEXT ROW: Bind off 2 sts, * turn, cast on 2 sts using cable cast-on method (see page 11), turn, pass second st on RH needle over first, pass third st on RH needle over first, bind off 2 sts, rep from * until all sts have been bound off.

ADD TOP PANEL

With RS facing and using size 3 (3mm) needles and A, with RS of work facing upward, pick up and k 61 sts along cast-on edge.

ROW I (WS): K3, p to last 3 sts, k3.

ROW 2: K to end of row.

Work the last 2 rows twice more and then rep Row 1 once more, ending with a WS row.

Cont in twisted stitch pattern.

ROW I (rS): * Skip first st, k into second st, k into first st, let 2 loops slip off LH needle tog; rep from * to last st, k1.

ROW 2: P to end of row.

Work the last 2 rows once more.

ROW I: K1, * skip first st, k into second st, k into first st, let 2 loops slip off LH needle tog; rep from * to end of row.

ROW 2: P to end of row.

Bind off knitwise.

TO MAKE THE RIGHT SIDE OF COLLAR

Work as given for Left Side, reversing all shaping.

TO MAKE THE BACK TIES (MAKE TWO)

Here are two different methods for making ties. Option A has been worked on Colorway 1, while Option B has been worked on Colorway 2.

OPTION A

Using size 3 (3mm) needles and A, cast on 7 sts using the lace cast-on method.

Work 7 sts in twisted stitch pattern as before until ties are 11¾" (30cm) long when slightly stretched. Bind off.

OPTION B

Using size 3 (3mm) needles and A, cast on 141 sts using the lace cast-on method.

ROW I: * Skip first st, knit into second st, knit into first st, let 2 loops slip off LH needle tog; rep from * to last st, k1.

ROW 2: P to end of row.

ROW 3: K1, * skip first st, knit into second st, knit into first st, let 2 loops slip off LH needle tog; rep from * to end of row.

Bind off purlwise.

TO MAKE THE COVERED BUTTON

Here are two different methods for covering buttons. Option A has been worked on Colorway 1, while Option B has been used on Colorway 2.

OPTION A

Using a self-cover button and a piece of your gauge swatch cut to slightly larger than the circumference on the button, cover the top surface of the button by catching the raw edges of the knitting and sew them together on the underside of the button. Work a round of buttonhole or blanket stitch around the circumference of the button.

OPTION B

Using either MC or A, work an extra tie. Coil the tie up tightly and stitch to secure. Work a round of buttonhole stitch around the circumference. Embroider several French knots all over the top surface of the button.

TO FINISH

Sew a tie at the top center back edge of each collar piece.
Embroider a row of French knots in yarn A along any of the twisted stitch rows on each side of the collar.
With right sides facing upward, lay the two halves of the collar together with the center fronts slightly overlapping at the top edge.
Sew the button securely in place to join the two halves of the collar at the center front.

LACE TOP
WITH BOW

 *learn*

SIZE

TO FIT BUST	30"	32"	34"	36"	38"
	76cm	81cm	86cm	91cm	97cm
ACTUAL BUST	32"	33½"	36"	37½"	39¾"
	81cm	85cm	91cm	95cm	101cm
LENGTH	18½"	19¼"	20"	21"	21½"
	47cm	49cm	51cm	53cm	55cm

YOU WILL NEED

A lightweight mohair yarn (3), such as Debbie Bliss
  Angel, in the following colors:
A 2 (2: 2: 2: 2) x ⅞-oz (25g) balls in off white (Ivory)
B 1 x ⅞-oz (25g) ball in mid pink (Coral)
C 1 x ⅞-oz (25g) ball in pale pink (Candyfloss)
Pair each of US sizes 6 and 7 (4mm and 4.5mm)
  knitting needles
Size D-3 (3.25mm) crochet hook (optional)

GAUGE

20 sts and 32 rows to 4" (10cm) square measured over
stockinette stitch using size 7 (4.5mm) needles. Adjust
needle size as necessary to obtain correct gauge.

ABBREVIATIONS

See standard abbreviations on page 9.

TO MAKE THE BACK

Using size 6 (4mm) needles and A, cast on 81 (85: 91: 95:
101) sts.
Beg with a k row, work in St st but AT THE SAME TIME
dec 1 st at each end of every 4th (4th: 5th: 5th: 5th) row
until there are 67 (71: 77: 81: 87) sts, changing to size 7
(4.5mm) needles after 32 rows have been worked.
Work even in St st for 20 (22: 16: 18: 19) rows.
Cont to work in St st but AT THE SAME TIME inc 1 st at
each end of every 5th (5th: 5th: 5th: 6th) row until there
are 81 (85: 91: 95: 101) sts.
Work even in St st for 7 (9: 10: 10: 6) rows, ending with a
WS row.

SHAPE ARMHOLES

Bind off 2 (2: 3: 3: 4) sts at beg of next 2 rows. *77 (81: 85:
89: 93) sts.*
Dec 1 st at each end of next 2 (3: 4: 5: 6) rows, then 2 (1:
1: 1: –) foll alt rows, then 1 (2: 1: 1: 1) foll 4th (3rd: 3rd:
5th: 3rd) rows, and then foll – (–: 5th: – 5th) row. *67 (69:
71: 75: 77) sts.* **

Work even in St st until Back measures 7¼ (7¾: 8: 8½:
8¾)"/18.5 (19.5: 20.5: 21.5: 22.5)cm from beg of armhole
shaping, ending with a WS row.

SHAPE BACK NECK AND SHOULDERS

NEXT ROW (RS): K 18 (19: 20: 22: 23) sts, turn, leave rem
unworked sts on a stitch holder.
Work each side of neck separately.
NEXT ROW: P3, p2tog, p to end of row. *17 (18: 19: 21: 22) sts.*
NEXT ROW (RS): Bind off 5 (5: 5: 6: 6) sts, knit to last 5 sts,
k2tog, k3. *11 (12: 13: 14: 15) sts.*
NEXT ROW: P to end of row.
NEXT ROW: Bind off 5 (5: 6: 6: 7) sts, knit to last 5 sts,
k2tog, k3. *5 (6: 6: 7: 7) sts.*
NEXT ROW: P to end of row.
Bind off rem 5 (6: 6: 7: 7) sts.
With RS facing, rejoin A to rem sts.
NEXT ROW: Bind off center 31 sts, k to end of row.

NOTE: Do not bind off the center stitches too tightly as the sides of the neck will pull inward.

Complete neck and shoulders to match first side, reversing all shaping.

QUATREFOIL LACE PATTERN (QF) USED ON FRONT (10-ROW REPEAT WORKED OVER 15 STS)

NOTE: As lace stitches are increased and decreased over the 10-row repeat lace pattern, do not count sts within this panel on the 6th, 7th, 8th or 9th rows.

ROW 1 (RS): K5, k2tog, yo, k1, yo, sl1, k1, psso, k5.
ROW 2: P4, p2tog tbl, yo, p3, yo, p2tog, p4.
ROW 3: K3, k2tog, yo, k5, yo, sl1, k1, psso, k3.
ROW 4: P2, p2tog tbl, yo, p1, yo, p2tog, p1, p2tog tbl, yo, p1, yo, p2tog, p2.
ROW 5: K1, k2tog, yo, k3, yo, k3tog, yo, k3, yo, sl1, k1, psso, k1.
ROW 6: P2, yo, p5, yo, p1, yo, p5, yo, p2.
ROW 7: [K3, yo, sl1, k1, psso, k1, k2tog, yo] twice, k3.
ROW 8: P4, p3tog, yo, p5, yo, p3tog, p4.
ROW 9: K6, yo, sl1, k1, psso, k1, k2tog, yo, k6.
ROW 10: P3, p2tog tbl, p2, yo, p3tog, yo, p2, p2tog, p3.
Repeat Rows 1–10 to form the pattern.

FANCY SHELL LACE PATTERN (FS) USED ON FRONT (4-ROW REPEAT WORKED OVER 9 STS)

ROW 1 (RS): P2, k1, [yo, k1] 4 times, p2.
ROW 2: K2, p1, [k1, p1] 4 times, k2.
ROW 3: P2, k1, p1, ssk, k1, k2tog, p1, k1, p2.
ROW 4: K2, p1, k1, p3tog, k1, p1, k2.
Repeat Rows 1–4 to form the pattern.

TO MAKE THE FRONT

Using size 6 (4mm) needles and A, cast on 81 (85: 91: 95: 101) sts.

ROW 1 (RS): K 20 (22: 25: 27: 30) in A, work 9 sts of Row 1 of FS pattern in B, k4 in A, work 15 sts of Row 1 of QF pattern in C, k4 in A, work 9 sts of Row 1 of FS pattern in B, k 20 (22: 25: 27: 30) in A.

NOTE: Link yarns when changing color along a row using the intarsia method to avoid a hole (see page 90).

This last row sets the position of the lace panels.

Cont to work in St st with inset lace panels in contrasting colors as set but AT THE SAME TIME work as given for Back to **. *67 (69: 71: 75: 77) sts.*

Work even in St st keeping inset lace panels correct as set until work measures 3½ (4: 4¼: 4¾: 5)"/9 (10: 11: 12: 13)cm from beg of armhole shaping, ending with a WS row.

SHAPE FRONT NECK

NEXT ROW (RS): K 13 (14: 15: 17: 18) in A, work 9 sts of FS pattern in B, k4 in A, work first 3 sts of QF pattern in C, turn and leave rem unworked sts on a stitch holder. Work each side of neck separately.

NEXT ROW (WS): Bind off 4 sts purlwise in C, p3 in A, work 9 sts of FS pattern in B, p to end in A. *25 (26: 27: 29: 30) sts.*

NOTE: Do not bind off the center stitches too tightly as the sides of the neck will pull inward.

Dec 1 st at neck edge of next 7 rows, then foll alt row, then foll 6th row, then foll 10th row. *15 (16: 17: 19: 20) sts.* Work even in pattern as set for 5 rows, ending with a WS row.

SHAPE SHOULDER

NEXT ROW (RS): Bind off 5 (5: 5: 6: 6) sts, pattern to end of row. *10 (11: 12: 13: 14) sts.*

NEXT ROW (WS): Pattern to end of row.

NEXT ROW (RS): Bind off 5 (5: 6: 6: 7) sts, pattern to end of row. *5 (6: 6: 7: 7) sts.*

NEXT ROW (WS): Pattern to end of row.

Bind off rem 5 (6: 6: 7: 7) sts.

With RS facing, rejoin C to rem sts.

NEXT ROW: Bind off center 9 sts, pattern to end of row.

NOTE: Do not bind off the center stitches too tightly as the sides of the neck will pull inward.

Complete to match first side of neck, reversing all shaping.

TO MAKE THE NECK TIE

Using size 6 (4mm) needles and B, cast on 9 sts.
ROW 1: K2, [p1, k1] 3 times, k1.
ROW 2: K1, [p1, k1] 4 times.
Repeat last 2 rows until Neck Tie measures 55" (140cm). Bind off.

TO FINISH

Sew shoulder seams.

Sew side seams using mattress stitch.

Place center of one side edge of Neck Tie at center back of neck, sew in position all around neck edge to outer edges of QF lace panel, leaving front bands free to tie in a bow.

ADD PICOT EDGES (OPTIONAL)

Using size D-3 (3.25mm) crochet hook and A, work along lower edge of top either into each stitch or into stitch loops between sts as foll: chain 3, 1 single crochet. Using C, repeat around both armhole edges.

"**THIS LACE TOP IS PERFECT FOR ALL SEASONS** and can be dressed up or down. Wear it on its own in summer, while in winter pair it with a cardigan or jacket. Once you have mastered both lace knitting and intarsia techniques in this lightweight knitted fabric, you too will want to jump for joy!"

RANDOM-STRIPED SWEATER

 learn

SIZE

TO FIT BUST	32"	34"	36"	38"	40"
	81cm	86cm	91cm	97cm	102cm
ACTUAL BUST	32½"	34½"	36½"	38½"	40½"
	83cm	88cm	93cm	98cm	103cm
LENGTH	18½"	19½"	20½"	21½"	22½"
	47cm	49.5cm	52cm	55.5	57.5cm
SLEEVE SEAM	18"	18¼"	18¼"	18¾"	18¾"
	45.5cm	46cm	46cm	47.5cm	47.5cm

YOU WILL NEED

A lightweight wool yarn (3), such as BC-Garn Semilla Organic DK, in the following colors:

FOR COLORWAY ONE
A 3 (4: 5: 5: 6) x 1¾-oz (50g) balls in mid blue (Teal)
B 1 x 1¾-oz (50g) ball in mustard (Relish)
C 1 x 1¾-oz (50g) ball in pale blue (Duck Egg Blue)
D 1 x 1¾-oz (50g) ball in pale purple (Wysteria)
E 1 x 1¾-oz (50g) ball in mid brown (Truffle Brown)
F 1 x 1¾-oz (50g) ball in deep pink (Rose)
G 1 x 1¾-oz (50g) ball in dark gray (Charcoal Grey)
H 1 x 1¾-oz (50g) ball in deep red (Plum Wine)
I 1 x 1¾-oz (50g) ball in mid purple (Lavender)
J 1 x 1¾-oz (50g) ball in turquoise (Turquoise)

FOR COLORWAY TWO
A 3 (4: 5: 5: 6) x 1¾-oz (50g) balls in lilac (Dusty Lilac)
B 1 x 1¾-oz (50g) ball in mauve (Mauve)
C 1 x 1¾-oz (50g) ball in pale gray (Light Grey)
D 1 x 1¾-oz (50g) ball in turquoise (Turquoise)
E 1 x 1¾-oz (50g) ball in mid green (Grass)
F 1 x 1¾-oz (50g) ball in deep pink (Rose)
G 1 x 1¾-oz (50g) ball in mid brown (Truffle Brown)
H 1 x 1¾-oz (50g) ball in deep purple (Deep Purple)
I 1 x 1¾-oz (50g) ball in bright purple (Bright Purple)
J 1 x 1¾-oz (50g) ball in pale purple (Wysteria)

Pair each of size US sizes 5 and 6 (3.75mm and 4mm) knitting needles
US size 5 (3.75mm) circular knitting needle

GAUGE

24 sts and 36 rows to 4" (10cm) square measured over stockinette stitch using size 6 (4mm) needles. Adjust needle size as necessary to obtain correct gauge.

ABBREVIATIONS

See standard abbreviations on page 9.

STRIPE SEQUENCE FOR COLORWAY ONE

**

Color	Rows		Color	Rows
F	3 rows		E	3 rows
G	1 row		F	1 row
D	2 rows		G	2 rows
J	4 rows		I	3 rows
H	2 rows		B	2 rows
B	1 row		H	1 row
A	3 rows		A	3 rows
C	1 row		G	3 rows
D	1 row		C	2 rows
E	2 rows		B	1 row
G	3 rows		D	2 rows
F	2 rows		E	2 rows
J	1 row		J	1 row
B	2 rows		H	2 rows
H	1 row		C	1 row
I	3 rows		F	2 rows
G	1 row		B	3 rows
C	2 rows		G	2 rows
E	3 rows		J	3 rows
F	2 rows		I	2 rows
B	3 rows		H	1 row
A	2 rows		E	1 row
H	1 row		A	2 rows
D	3 rows		B	1 row
G	2 rows		D	3 rows
J	3 rows		A	1 row
E	2 rows		F	2 rows
B	2 rows		C	3 rows
C	1 row		E	3 rows
H	2 rows		H	2 rows
I	1 row		B	3 rows
G	1 row		G	1 row
A	2 rows		J	2 rows
B	1 row		F	1 row
F	4 rows		I	3 rows
C	2 rows		H	1 row
J	3 rows		C	2 rows
D	2 rows		A	4 rows

repeat from **

STRIPE SEQUENCE FOR COLORWAY TWO

**

Color	Rows		Color	Rows
F	3 rows		F	2 rows
D	2 rows		I	2 rows
E	1 row		E	2 rows
C	3 rows		C	3 rows
G	2 rows		H	1 row
B	2 rows		J	1 row
E	2 rows		G	4 rows
A	3 rows		B	2 rows
H	2 rows		E	1 row
F	1 row		D	3 rows
I	3 rows		H	2 rows
C	4 rows		A	3 rows
J	2 rows		I	4 rows
D	3 rows		G	2 rows
H	1 row		J	3 rows
B	3 rows		F	3 rows
F	2 rows		C	4 rows
I	1 row		B	3 rows
G	2 rows		H	1 row
E	3 rows		J	1 row
A	4 rows		E	2 rows
H	2 rows		A	2 rows
J	3 rows		I	3 rows
C	4 rows		H	1 row
D	2 rows		F	1 row
I	1 row		G	2 rows
A	2 rows		D	3 rows
F	3 rows		B	2 rows
G	2 rows		E	1 row
H	1 row		J	3 rows
E	2 rows		F	2 rows
B	3 rows		H	2 rows
A	1 row		C	3 rows
J	3 rows		I	3 rows

repeat from **

TO MAKE THE BACK

Using size 5 (3.75mm) needles and B, cast on 82 (88: 94: 100. 106) sts.

ROW 1 (RS): * K1, p1; rep from * to end of row..

ROW 2: * K1, p1; rep from * to end of row.

The last 2 rows form the single rib (k1, p1 rib) pattern.
Cont to work in single rib as set for 12 rows more, ending with a WS row.

Change to size 6 (4mm) needles and F.

ROW 1 (INC): K3, M1, knit to last 3 sts, M1, k3.

ROW 2: P to end of row.

Work even in St st for 8 rows but AT THE SAME TIME foll stripe sequence.

Cont to work in St st but inc 1 st at each end of next and every 10th row as set but AT THE SAME TIME foll stripe sequence until 90 (100: 108: 118: 126) rows have been worked. *100 (106: 112: 118: 124) sts.*

SHAPE ARMHOLES

Keeping stripe sequence correct, bind off 4 (4: 4: 6: 6) sts at beg of next 2 rows. *92 (98: 104: 106: 112) sts.*

NEXT ROW: K1, skp, k to last 3 sts, k2tog, k1.

NEXT ROW: P to end of row.

Rep last 2 rows until 58 (64: 70: 70: 76) sts rem. **
Keeping stripe sequence correct, work even in St st for 24 rows.

NEXT ROW (RS): K12 (15: 18: 18: 21), k2tog, turn, leave rem unworked sts on a stitch holder.

NEXT ROW: K2tog, p to end of row.

NEXT ROW (RS): Bind off 6 (7: 9: 9: 10) sts at shoulder edge.

NEXT ROW: P to end of row.

Bind off rem 6 (8: 9: 9: 11) sts.

Leaving center 30 sts on a stitch holder, with RS facing rejoin yarn at neck edge.

NEXT ROW (RS): K2tog, k to end.

NEXT ROW: P to last 2 sts, k2tog.

NEXT ROW: K to end of row.

NEXT ROW: Bind off 6 (7: 9: 9: 10) sts, p to end of row.
Bind off rem 6 (8: 9: 9: 11) sts.

TO MAKE THE FRONT

Work as given for Back to **.
Work each side of neck separately.

ROW 1 (RS): K17 (20: 23: 23: 26), k2tog, turn, leave rem unworked sts on a stitch holder.

ROW 2: P to end of row.

Rep last 2 rows until 12 (15: 18: 18: 21) sts rem.

Keeping stripe sequence correct, work even in St st for 12 rows.

NEXT ROW: Bind off 6 (7: 9: 9: 10) sts.

NEXT ROW: P to end of row.

Bind off rem 6 (8: 9: 9: 11) sts.

Leaving center 20 sts on a stitch holder, with RS facing rejoin yarn at neck edge.

Complete right side of neck to match left side, reversing all shaping.

TO MAKE THE SLEEVES (MAKE TWO)

Using size size 5 (3.75mm) needles and B, cast on 48 (54: 60: 66: 72) sts

ROW 1 (RS): * K1, p1; rep from * to end of row.

ROW 2: * K1, p1; rep from * to end of row.

The last 2 rows form the single rib (k1, p1 rib) pattern.
Cont to work in single rib as set for 12 rows more, ending with a WS row.

Change to size 6 (4mm) needles and A.

Beg with a k row, work in St st but AT THE SAME TIME inc 1 st at each end of next and every 10th row until there are 74 (80: 86: 92: 98) sts.

Work even in St st until Sleeve measures 17¾ (18: 18½: 19: 19¼)"/45 (46: 47: 48: 49)cm from cast-on edge.

Bind off 4 (4: 4: 6: 6) sts at beg of next 2 rows. *66 (72: 78: 80: 86) sts.*

NEXT ROW: K1, skp, k to last 3 sts, k2tog, k1.

Work even in St st for 3 rows.

Rep last 4 rows 9 times more. *46 (52: 58: 60: 66) sts.*

NEXT ROW: K1, skp, k to last 3 sts, k2tog, k1.

NEXT ROW: K to end of row.

Rep last 2 rows until 36 (42: 48: 50: 56) sts rem.

Bind off 3 sts at beg of next 6 rows.

Bind off rem 18 (24: 30: 32: 38) sts.

TO FINISH

Weave in any loose yarn ends.

Sew shoulder seams using backstitch.

Using size 5 (3.75mm) circular needle and B, with RS facing and starting at left shoulder seam, pick up and k 24 sts down left front neck, k 20 sts from stitch holder at center front neck, pick up and k 24 sts up right front neck to right shoulder seam and 5 sts down back right neck, k 30 sts from stitch holder at center back neck, and pick up and k 5 sts up back left neck. *108 sts.*

Working in rounds, work 6 rounds in single rib (k1, p1 rib).
Bind off loosely in rib.

love TO KNIT

COLLEGE-STYLE CARDIGAN
WITH PATCH POCKET

SIZE

TO FIT BUST	32"	34"	36"	38"	40"
	81cm	86cm	91cm	97cm	102cm
ACTUAL BUST	32"	34"	36"	38"	40"
	81cm	86cm	91cm	97cm	102cm
LENGTH	16½"	17"	17¾"	18½"	19"
	42cm	43.5cm	45cm	47cm	48.5cm
SLEEVE SEAM	17¼"	17½"	17¾"	18"	18¼"
	44cm	44.5cm	45cm	45.5cm	46cm

YOU WILL NEED

A super fine wool yarn (**1**), such as Jamieson's Spindrift, in the following colors:
- **A** 3 (4: 5: 6: 7) x ⅞-oz (25g) balls in red (Poppy)
- **B** 5 (6: 7: 8: 9) x ⅞-oz (25g) balls in beige (Eesit)

Pair each of US sizes 2 and 3 (2.75mm and 3.25mm) knitting needles
10 small buttons, ½" (1.5cm) in diameter

"**WITH ITS SHORT AND SNUGGLY FITTED SHAPE,** worked in tweedy Shetland yarn with tiny buttons running up the front, this preppy, college-style cardigan brings together the worlds of traditional British handknitting and American varsity jackets. This cardigan is partly knitted in a simple twist stitch, which gives the fabric a really lovely texture.**"**

GAUGE

24 sts and 34 rows to 4" (10cm) square measured over stockinette stitch using size 3 (3.25mm) needles. Adjust needle size as necessary to obtain correct gauge.

ABBREVIATIONS

twist 2—ignore first stitch, knit into second stitch, knit into first stitch, drop both stitches off the needle together (see instructions on page 86 for working this twist stitch pattern).
See also standard abbreviations on page 9.

PATTERN NOTES

The twist stitch pattern is always worked in A, while the stockinette stitch is always worked in B. Link yarns when changing color to avoid a hole.

TO MAKE THE BACK

Using size 2 (2.75mm) needles and B, cast on 91 (97: 103: 109: 115) sts.

ROW 1 (RS): * K2, p2; rep from * to last 3 (1: 3: 1: 3) sts, k 2 (1: 2: 1: 2), p 1 (–: 1: –: 1).

ROW 2: K 1 (–: 1: –: 1), p 2 (1: 2: 1: 2), * k2, p2; rep from * to end of row.

The last 2 rows form the double rib (k2, p2 rib) pattern.

Cont to work in double rib as set for 12 rows more, ending with a WS row.

Change to size 3 (3.25mm) needles and A, then cont as foll:

ROW 1 (RS): K1, * twist 2, k1; rep from * to end of row.

ROW 2: P to end of row.

The last 2 rows form the twist stitch pattern.

Cont to work in twist stitch as set for 22 rows more, ending with a WS row.

SHAPE SIDES

Cont to work in twist stitch but AT THE SAME TIME inc 1 st at each end of next and every foll 18th (18th: 19th: 20th: 20th) row, taking inc sts into patt, until there are 97 (103: 109: 115: 121) sts.

Work even in twist stitch until Back measures 8½ (8¾: 9: 9½: 9¾)"/22 (22.5: 23: 24: 24.5)cm from cast-on edge, ending with a WS row.

Using B and beg with a k row, work 4 rows in St st.

Using A, work 6 rows in twist stitch.

SHAPE ARMHOLES

Using B only, cont to work in St st but AT THE SAME TIME shape armholes as foll:

Bind off 4 (5: 5: 6: 6) sts at beg of next 2 rows.

Dec 1 st at each end of next 4 (5: 5: 6: 6) rows and then 2 (2: 3: 3: 4) foll alt rows. *77 (79: 83: 85: 89) sts.*

Work even in St st until Back measures 16½ (17¼: 17¾: 18½: 19)"/42 (43.5: 45: 47: 48.5)cm from cast-on edge, ending with a WS row.

SHAPE SHOULDERS AND BACK NECK

NEXT ROW (RS): Bind off 6 (7: 7: 8: 8) sts, k until there are 17 (17: 19: 19: 21) sts on RH needle, turn, leave rem unworked sts on a stitch holder.

Work each side of neck separately.

Bind off 2 sts at beg of next row, bind off 7 (7: 8: 8: 9) sts at beg of foll row, then dec 1 st at beg of foll row.

Bind off rem 7 (7: 8: 8: 9) sts.

With RS facing, rejoin A to rem sts from stitch holder.

NEXT ROW (RS): Bind off center 31 sts, k to end of row.

NEXT ROW (WS): Bind off 6 (7: 7: 8: 8) sts, p to end of row. *17 (17: 19: 19: 21) sts.*

Complete to match first side of neck, reversing all shaping.

TO MAKE THE LEFT FRONT

Using size 2 (2.75mm) needles and B, cast on 49 (52: 55: 58: 61) sts.

ROW 1 (RS): P1, k2 (k2: k1: –: p1, k2), * p2, k2; rep from * to last 6 sts, [k1, p1] 3 times.

ROW 2: [P1, k1] 3 times, * p2, k2; rep from * to last 3 (2: 1: –: 3) sts, p2, k1 (p2: p1: –: p2, k1).

The last 2 rows form the double rib (k2, p2 rib) pattern with a 6 seed stitch band at front edge.

Cont to work in double rib with seed stitch band as set for 11 rows more, ending with a RS row.

NEXT ROW (WS): Work 6 sts in seed st and slip onto a stitch holder or safety pin, rib to end of row. *43 (46: 49: 52: 55) sts on needle.*

Change to size 3 (3.25mm) needles and A, then cont as foll:

ROW 1 (RS): K1, * twist 2, k1; rep from * to end of row.

ROW 2: P to end of row.

The last 2 rows form the twist stitch pattern.

Cont to work in twist stitch as set for 22 rows more, ending with a WS row.

SHAPE SIDES

Cont to work in twist stitch but AT THE SAME TIME inc 1 st at side edge of next and every foll 18th (18th: 19th: 20th: 20th) row, taking inc sts into patt, until there are 46 (49: 52: 55: 58) sts.

Work even in twist stitch until Left Front matches Back to beg of armhole shaping, ending with a WS row.

SHAPE ARMHOLE

Cont to work in twist stitch but AT THE SAME TIME shape armholes as foll:

Bind off 4 (5: 5: 6: 6) sts at beg of next row.

Work even in twist stitch for 1 row.

Dec 1 st at armhole edge of next 4 (5: 5: 6: 6) rows and then 2 (2: 3: 3: 4) foll alt rows. *36 (37: 39: 40: 42) sts.*

Work even in twist stitch for 5 (7: 5: 7: 7) rows, ending with a RS (WS: WS: RS: RS) row.

Cont to work even but AT THE SAME TIME work diagonal shoulder stripes using A and B, maintaining vertical continuity of twist stitch in main panel, as foll:

ROW 1: Using B work 1 st in St st at armhole edge—so for this Row 1 it is the last (first: first: last: last) st—then using A work remainder of row in twist stitch.

Work an additional 1 st in St st using B at armhole edge

than on the preceding row on next 3 rows until 4 sts are worked in B at armhole edge.

NOTE: The overall number of stitches remains the same but more B sts and fewer A sts are worked on each row.

ROW 5: Using A work 1 st in twist st at armhole edge, then using B work 4 sts in St st, then using A work remainder of row in twist stitch.

Work an additional 1 st in twist st using A at armhole edge than on the preceding row on next 5 rows until 6 sts are worked in A at armhole edge.

NOTE: The overall number of stitches remains the same but the 4-st stripe worked in B moves position on each row toward the front edge.

ROW 11: Using B work 1 st in St st at armhole edge, then using A work 6 sts in twist st, then using B work 4 sts in St st, then using A work remainder of row in twist stitch.

Work an additional 1 st in St st using B at armhole edge than on preceding row, adjusting the position of both A and B stripes on all subsequent rows, until 10 sts are worked in A at front edge, ending with a RS row.

SHAPE NECK

Cont to work in pattern as set, adjusting position of stripes on each subsequent row, but AT THE SAME TIME shape neck as foll:

NEXT ROW (WS): Bind off 6 sts, pattern to end of row.
NEXT ROW: Pattern to end of row.
NEXT ROW (WS): Bind off 3 sts, pattern to end of row.
NEXT ROW: Pattern to end of row.
NEXT ROW (WS): Bind off 2 sts, pattern to end of row.
NEXT ROW: Pattern to end of row.

Cont to work in pattern as set but AT THE SAME TIME dec 1 st at neck edge of next 3 rows, and then 2 foll 4th rows. *20 (21: 23: 24: 26) sts.*

NOTE: During the neck shaping the stripes will reach the front neck edge, at which point work in St st using B only. Work even in St st until Left Front measures same as Back to start of shoulder shaping, ending with a WS row.

SHAPE SHOULDERS

Bind off 6 (7: 7: 8: 8) sts at beg of next row and .
Work 1 row.
Bind off 7 (7: 8: 8: 9) sts at beg of next row.
Work 1 row.
Bind off rem 7 (7: 8: 8: 9) sts.

TO MAKE THE RIGHT FRONT

Using size 2 (2.75mm) needles and B, cast on 49 (52: 55: 58: 61) sts.

ROW 1 (RS): [K1, p1] 3 times, * k2, p2; rep from * to last 3 (2: 1: –: 3) sts, k2, p1 (k2: k1: –: k2, p1).

ROW 2 (WS): K1, p2 (p2: p1: –: k1, p2), * k2, p2; rep from * to last 6 sts, [p1, k1] 3 times.

The last 2 rows form the double rib (k2, p2 rib) pattern with a 6 seed stitch band at front edge.

Cont to work in double rib with seed stitch band as set for 2 rows more, ending with a WS row.

BUTTONHOLE ROW (RS): Work 3 sts in seed st, yo, k2tog, pattern to end of row.

Cont to work in double rib with seed stitch band as set for 7 rows more, ending with a WS row.

NEXT ROW (RS): Work 6 sts in seed st and slip onto a stitch holder or safety pin, rib to end of row. *43 (46: 49: 52: 55) sts on needle.*

Cont to work in double rib for 1 row more.

Change to size 3 (3.25mm) needles and A, then cont to work as given for Left Front, reversing all shaping.

TO MAKE THE SLEEVES (MAKE TWO)

Using size 2 (2.75mm) needles and A, cast on 51 (53: 55: 57: 59) sts.

Work in double rib (k2, p2 rib) as given for Back but AT THE SAME TIME inc 1 st at each end of 6th (6th: 6th: 5th: 5th) row and every foll 6th (6th: 6th: 5th: 5th) row until there are 59 (61: 63: 67: 69) sts.

Cont to work in double rib until Sleeve measures 3¼" (8cm) from cast on edge, ending with a WS row.

Change to size 3 (3.25mm) needles and B, then beg with a k row, work 4 rows in St st.

Change to A, then cont as foll:

FOR 1ST SIZE ONLY

ROW 1 (RS): K2, twist 2, * k1, twist 2; rep from * to last st, k1.

ROW 2: P to end of row.

FOR 2ND AND 4TH SIZES ONLY

ROW 1 (RS): * K1, twist 2; rep from * to last st, k1.
ROW 2: P to end of row.

FOR 3RD AND 5TH SIZES ONLY

ROW 1 (RS): * K1, twist 2; rep from * to end of row.
ROW 2: P to end of row.

The last 2 rows form the twist stitch pattern.

Cont to work in twist stitch as set for 4 rows more, ending with a WS row.

Change to B and beg with a k row, work 2 (2: 3: 3: 3) rows in St st.

WORKING THE TWIST STITCH

"The red sections of this garment are mostly knitted using a simple twist stitch, which is a 3-stitch repeat pattern. The twist stitch is based on the same principle as any cable stitch, however, as the twists are so small— with only two stitches to each twist—this technique can be executed without the use of a cable needle."

STEP 1 The first stitch in the 3-stitch repeat pattern is knitted as usual, while the next 2 stitches are twisted. For "twist 2," ignore the first stitch on the left-hand needle and insert the right-hand needle up into the second stitch on the left needle.

STEP 2 Wrap the yarn around the needle from back to front and pull the yarn through the stitch with the right-hand needle, but do not slide the stitch off the left-hand needle yet as you would if you were knitting the stitch normally.

STEP 3 With the new loop still on the right-hand needle, knit into the first stitch on the left-hand needle previously ignored. Wrap the yarn around the needle from back to front and bring through to create another loop on your right-hand needle.

STEP 4 With these two new loops on the right-hand needle, gently slide both of the stitches that you have just knitted off the left-hand needle.

SHAPE SIDES

Cont to work in St st but AT THE SAME TIME inc 1 st at each end of next and every foll 13th row until there are 77 (79: 81: 85: 87) sts.

Work even in St st until Sleeve measures 17¼ (17½: 17¾: 18: 18¼)"/44 (44.5: 45: 45.5: 46)cm from cast-on edge, ending with a WS row.

SHAPE TOP OF SLEEVE

Bind off 4 sts at beg of next 2 rows. *69 (71: 73: 77: 79) sts.*
Dec 1 st at each end of next 4 rows, then on 4 foll alt rows, then on foll 4th row.

Dec 1 st at each end of foll 8th (9th: 10th: 12th: 14th) row, foll 7th (9th: 10th: 12th: 14th) row, then foll 4th row.

Dec 1 st at each end of 3 (2: 1: 1: –) foll alt rows, then next 5 (8: 10: 8: 10) rows.

FOR 4TH AND 5TH SIZES ONLY

Bind off 4 sts at beg of next 2 rows.

ALL SIZES

Bind off rem 29 (27: 27: 27: 27) sts.

TO MAKE THE PATCH POCKET

Using size 3 (3.25mm) needles and B, cast on 20 sts.
Work in St st until Pocket measures 2¾" (7cm) from cast-on edge, ending with a WS row.

Change to size 2 (2.75mm) needles and work in double rib (k2, p2 rib) as given for Back until work measures 3½" (8.5cm) from cast-on edge.
Bind off in rib.

TO FINISH

Sew shoulder seams using backstitch.

WORK BUTTON BAND

With RS facing, slip 6 sts from Left Front stitch holder onto size 2 (2.75mm) needles and rejoin B.

Cont to work in seed st as set until button band stretches up Left Front to neck shaping, ending with a WS row.
Place 6 sts on a safety pin.
Slip stitch button band in place.
Mark position of 10 buttons on Left Front button band. The last button must correspond to buttonhole already worked in Right Front buttonhole band. The first button must sit just above the neck shaping within the neck band that is yet to be worked. Evenly space the remaining 8 buttons between these two buttons.

WORK BUTTONHOLE BAND

With WS facing, slip 6 sts from Right Front stitch holder onto size 2 (2.75mm) needles and rejoin yarn B.

Cont to work in seed st as set until buttonhole band stretches up Right Front to neck shaping, ending with a WS row but AT THE SAME TIME work 8 buttonholes to correspond with the marked positions on the button band as foll:

BUTTONHOLE ROW (RS): Work 3 sts in seed st, yo, k2tog, seed st to end of row.
Place 6 sts on a safety pin.
Slip stitch buttonhole band in place.

WORK NECK BAND

With RS facing and B, seed st 6 sts from stitch holder with buttonhole band sts, pick up and k 44 (45: 45: 48: 48) sts up right side of neck, 40 (42: 42: 44: 44) sts across Back neck, and 44 (45: 45: 48: 48) sts down left side of neck, then seed st 6 sts from stitch holder with button band sts. *140 (144: 144: 152: 152) sts.*

Cont to work in seed st as set for 3 rows more.

BUTTONHOLE ROW (RS): Work 3 sts in seed st, yo, k2tog, seed st to end of row.

Cont to work in seed st as set for 4 rows more, ending with a RS row.
Bind off in seed st.
Set in the sleeves, matching the center points of the top of the sleeves to the shoulder seams.
Sew side and sleeve seams.
Slip stitch the patch pocket in place on the Left Front.
Sew the buttons securely onto the Left Front button band to correspond with Right Front buttonholes.

SHAWL COLLAR CARDIGAN
WITH FLORAL EMBROIDERY

SIZE

TO FIT BUST	30"	32"	34"	36"	38"
	76cm	81cm	86cm	91cm	97cm
ACTUAL BUST	30¼"	32"	34¼"	36"	38"
	77cm	81cm	87cm	91cm	97cm
LENGTH	18¾"	19¼"	19¾"	20¼"	21"
	47.5cm	49cm	50cm	51.5cm	53.5cm
SLEEVE SEAM	17¼"	17½"	17¾"	18"	18¼"
	44cm	44.5cm	45cm	45.5cm	46cm

YOU WILL NEED

A fine-weight yarn (2), such as Blue Sky Alpaca Melange or Blue Sky Alpaca Sport Weight, in the following colors:
MC 8 (9: 10: 11: 12) x 1¾-oz (50g) hanks in mid blue (Melange, Cornflower)
A 1 x 1¾-oz (50g) hank in mustard (Melange, Dijon)
B 1 x 1¾-oz (50g) hank in bright pink (Sport Weight, Hibiscus)
Small amounts of tapestry wool or similar wool yarn, such as Laine St Pierre Darning Wool, in the following colors:
C gold (Mustard)
D off white (Almond)
E dark red (Garnet)
F mauve (Violet)
G dusky pink (Dusky Pink)
H dark blue (Petrol)
I bright green (Pistachio)
Pair each of US sizes 3 and 5 (3mm and 3.75mm) knitting needles
5 buttons

GAUGE

20 sts and 30 rows to 4" (10cm) square measured over stockinette stitch using size 5 (3.75mm) needles. Adjust needle size as necessary to obtain correct gauge.

ABBREVIATIONS

See standard abbreviations on page 9.

PATTERN NOTE

The floral motif on the Left and Right Fronts can be worked either integrally into the knitting using the intarsia method (see page 90) or embroidered onto the surface of the finished piece using duplicate stitch (see page 129).

TO MAKE THE BACK

Using size 5 (3.75mm) needles and MC, cast on 73 (77: 83: 87: 93) sts.
ROW 1 (RS): * K2, p2; rep from * to last st, k1.
ROW 2: P1, * k2, p2; rep from * to end of row.
The last 2 rows form the double rib (k2, p2 rib) pattern.
Cont to work in double rib as set for 12 rows more.
Change to size 3 (3mm) needles.
Cont to work in double rib for 16 rows more, inc 4 sts evenly across the last row. *77 (81: 87: 91: 97) sts.*
Change to size 5 (3.75mm) needles.
Beg with a k row, work in St st until Back measures 10¾ (11: 11: 11¼: 11)"/27.5 (28: 28: 28.5: 29.5)cm, ending with a WS row, but AT THE SAME TIME inc 1 st at each end of 3rd and every foll 24th (16th: 24th: 16th: 18th) row until there are 81 (87: 91: 97: 103) sts.

SHAPE ARMHOLES
Bind off 5 (5: 5: 6: 7) sts at beg of next 2 rows.
71 (77: 81: 85: 89) sts.
Dec 1 st at each end of next 3 (3: 3: 3: 5) rows.
65 (71: 75: 79: 79) sts.
Dec 1 st at each end of foll 1 (2: 3: 3: 2) alt rows.
63 (67: 69: 73: 75) sts.
Work even in St st until Back measures 18¾ (19¼: 19¾: 20¼: 21)"/47.5 (49: 50: 51.5: 53.5)cm from cast-on edge, ending with a WS row.

MAKING BOBBINS OF YARN AND WORKING MOTIFS IN INTARSIA

"When working in motifs in color, it is advisable to wind the different color yarns into separate small bobbins. If you work with whole balls, the yarns will twist together and you will inevitably spend lots of your knitting time untangling threads. Bobbins are easily made by hand. With these made, you can then go on to work blocks or motifs in color within your knitting, using the intarsia method whereby the different color yarns are linked with a simple twist."

STEP 1 With the tail end of the yarn in the palm of your hand, wrap the yarn in a figure eight around your thumb and either your index finger or little finger. The tail end of the yarn will be joined into your work and will be knitted from it this way.

STEP 2 Continue wrapping the yarn into a figure eight between your thumb and fingers until you have a large enough bobbin to complete the color area you are going to knit.

STEP 3 Once large enough, slide the yarn off your hand and cut off the yarn. Wrap the end tightly around the center of the bobbin to secure it and tuck in the end. Pull gently on the tail end in the center of the bobbin to ensure the yarn runs smoothly.

STEP 4 To change color on a knit row, lay the new color over the existing color and between the two needles, with the tail end to the left. Bring the new color under and then over the existing color. Knit the stitch with the new color.

STEP 5 Go back and pull gently on the tail end to tighten up the first stitch in the new color after you have worked a few more stitches.

SHAPE SHOULDERS AND BACK NECK

NEXT ROW (RS): Bind off 5 (6: 6: 6: 7) sts, k until there are 14 (14: 15: 16: 16) sts on RH needle, turn, leave rem unworked sts on a stitch holder.

Work each side of the neck separately.

Bind off 2 sts at beg of next row. *12 (12: 13: 14: 14) sts.*

Bind off 5 (6: 6: 7: 6) sts at beg of next row. *7 (6: 7: 7: 8) sts.*

Dec 1 st at beg of next row. *6 (5: 6: 6: 7) sts.*

Bind off rem 6 (5: 6: 6: 7) sts.

With RS facing, rejoin yarn MC to rem sts.

NEXT ROW (RS): Bind off center 25 (27: 27: 29: 29) sts, k to end of row.

NEXT ROW: Bind off 5 (6: 6: 6: 7) sts, p to end of row. *14 (14: 15: 16: 16) sts.*

Complete to match first side of neck, reversing all shaping.

TO MAKE LEFT FRONT

Using size 5 (3.75mm) and MC, cast on 40 (42: 45: 47: 50) sts.

ROW I (RS): K 0 (0: 1: 0: 0), p 2 (0: 2: 1: 0), * k2, p2; rep from * to last 2 sts, k2.

The last row forms the double rib (k2, p2 rib) pattern.

Cont to work in double rib as set for 13 rows more, ending with a WS row.

Change to size 3 (3mm) needles.

Cont to work in double rib as set for 15 rows more, ending with a RS row.

NEXT ROW (WS): P2, k2, p2, place sts just worked on a stitch holder or safety pin, k2, M1, work in rib as set to last 2 sts, M1, rib to end of row. *36 (38: 41: 43: 46) sts, not including 6 sts on stitch holder.*

Change to size 5 (3.75mm) needles.

Beg with a k row, work in St st from chart A on page 95 (if working floral motif in intarsia instead of in duplicate stitch) over the first 31 sts in the row, introducing yarns A and B where required, but AT THE SAME TIME inc 1 st at beg of 5th row and then at beg of 1 (2: 1: 2: 2) foll 24th (16th: 24th: 16th: 18th) rows. *38 (41: 43: 46: 49) sts.*

SHAPE FRONT SLOPE

Keeping floral motif correct (if working in intarsia), dec 1 st at center front edge of next and every foll 6th (6th: 6th: 5th: 5th) row until Left Front matches Back to beg of armhole shaping, ending with a WS row. *35 (38: 41: 44: 47) sts.*

SHAPE ARMHOLE

NEXT ROW (RS): Bind off 5 (5: 5: 6: 7) sts at beg of row and dec 1 (–: 1: 1: –) sts at end of row. *29 (33: 35: 37: 40) sts.*

Work 1 row.

Dec 1 st at armhole edge of next 3 (3: 3: 3: 5) rows, then on 1 (2: 3: 3: 2) foll alt rows but AT THE SAME TIME dec 1 st at center front edge as set on every foll 6th (6th: 6th: 5th: 5th) row since previous dec until 16 (17: 18: 19: 20) sts rem.

Work even until Left Front matches Back to beg of shoulder shaping, ending with a WS row.

SHAPE SHOULDER

Bind off 5 (6: 6: 6: 7) sts at beg of next row.

Work 1 row.

Bind off 5 (6: 6: 7: 6) sts at beg of next row.

Work 1 row.

Bind off rem 6 (5: 6: 6: 7) sts.

TO MAKE RIGHT FRONT

Using size 5 (3.75mm) needles and MC, cast on 40 (42: 45: 47: 50) sts.

ROW I (RS): * K2, p2; rep from * to last 0 (2: 1: 3: 2) sts, k 0 (2: 1: 2: 2), p 0 (0: 0: 1: 0).

ROW 2: K 0 (0: 0: 1: 0), p 0 (2: 1: 2: 2), * k2, p2; rep from * to end of row.

ROW 3 (BUTTONHOLE): K2, bind off next 2 sts, rib as set to end of row.

ROW 4 (BUTTONHOLE): K 0 (0: 0: 1: 0), p 0 (2: 1: 2: 2), * k2, p2; rep from * to last 2 sts, cast on 2 sts over those bound off in previous row (see page 63), p2.

Cont to work in double rib as set for 10 rows more.

Change to size 3 (3mm) needles.

Cont to work in double rib as set for 4 rows more.

Repeat Rows 3 and 4 to make a second buttonhole.

Cont to work in double rib as set for 9 rows more.

NEXT ROW (WS): Rib 2 sts as set, M1, rib as set to last 8 sts, M1, rib as set to end of row. *42 (44: 47: 49: 52) sts.*

NEXT ROW (RS): Rib 6 sts as set, place sts just worked on a stitch holder or safety pin, change to size 5 (3.75mm) needles and k to end of row. *36 (38: 41: 43: 46) sts, not including 6 sts on stitch holder.*

Cont to work in St st as given for Left Front, following chart B (if working floral motif in intarsia instead of in duplicate stitch) and reversing all shaping.

ADD SURFACE EMBROIDERY TO LEFT AND RIGHT FRONTS

Using duplicate stitch (see page 129) and yarns A and B, embroider the floral motifs on the Left and Right Fronts following charts A and B on pages 94 and 95.

Using a combination of cross-stitch in yarns C and D and French knots in yarns E, F, and G, work additional surface embroidery around the mustard and pink floral

motifs. Using whipped backstitch in yarns H and I, work additional surface embroidery to add stems to the flowers.

TO MAKE THE SLEEVES (MAKE TWO)
Using size 3 (3mm needles) and MC, cast on 41 (43: 45: 47: 49) sts.
Work 16 rows in double rib (k2, p2 rib) as given for 3rd (4th: 3rd: 4th: 3rd) size for Left Front.
Change to size 5 (3.75mm) needles and beg with a k row, work in St st but AT THE SAME TIME inc 1 st at each end of next row and 3 foll alt rows. *49 (51: 53: 55: 57) sts.*
Work even in St st for 2 rows.
Cont to work in St st but AT THE SAME TIME inc 1 st at each end of next row and every foll 13th (12th: 11th: 10th: 9th) row until there are 65 (69: 73: 77: 81) sts.
Work even in St st until Sleeve measures 17¼ (17½: 17¾: 18: 18¼)"/44 (44.5: 45: 45.5: 46)cm, ending with a WS row.

SHAPE TOP OF SLEEVE
Bind off 5 (5: 5: 6: 7) sts at beg of next 2 rows. *55 (59: 63: 65: 67) sts.*
Cont to work in St st but AT THE SAME TIME dec 1 st at each end of rows as foll:

FOR 1ST SIZE ONLY
next 3 rows, 3 foll alt rows, foll 4th row, foll 5th row, foll 4th row, foll 5th row, foll alt row, foll 3rd row, 3 foll alt rows, next 2 rows. *21 sts.*

FOR 2ND SIZE ONLY
next 4 rows, 2 foll 3rd rows, 2 foll 4th rows, foll 5th row, 2 foll 4th rows, foll 3rd row, 3 foll alt rows, next row, then bind off 3 sts at beg of next 2 rows. *21 sts.*

FOR 3RD SIZE ONLY
next 4 rows, foll 3rd row, foll 4th row, 2 foll 6th rows, foll 7th row, foll 4th row, 3 foll alt rows, next 4 rows, then bind off 4 sts at beg of next 2 rows. *21 sts.*

FOR 4TH SIZE ONLY
next 4 rows, foll 3rd row, foll 4th row, 2 foll 7th rows, foll 5th row, foll 4th row, 5 foll alt rows, next 3 rows, then bind off 4 sts at beg of next 2 rows. *21 sts.*

FOR 5TH SIZE ONLY
next 5 rows, foll 4th row, 2 foll 8th rows, foll 7th row, foll 5th row, foll 3rd row, 3 foll alt rows, next 2 rows, then bind off 3 sts at beg of next 2 rows and bind off 4 sts at beg of next 2 rows. *21 sts.*

ALL SIZES
Bind off rem 21 sts.

TO FINISH
Sew shoulder seams using backstitch.

WORK LEFT FRONT BUTTON BAND AND COLLAR
Using size 3 (3mm) needles and with RS facing, rejoin yarn MC to 6 sts held on stitch holder at Left Front.
Work 4 rows in double rib as set.
Cont to work in double rib as set but AT THE SAME TIME inc 1 st at end of next and every foll 8th row until there are 12 sts, incorporating all inc sts into double rib.
Then inc 1 st at end of every foll 4th until there are 18 sts.
Then inc 1 st at end of every alt row until there are 38 sts.
Work even in double rib as set until button band and collar when slightly stretched reaches center back neck.
Bind off in rib.

WORK RIGHT FRONT BUTTONHOLE BAND AND COLLAR
Using size 3 (3mm) needles and with WS facing, rejoin yarn MC to 6 sts held on stitch holder at Right Front.
Work 1 row in k2, p2 rib as set.
ROW I (BUTTONHOLE): K2, bind off next 2 sts, k to end of row.
ROW 2 (BUTTONHOLE): P2, cast on 2 sts over those bound off in previous row, p2.
Cont to work in double rib as set but AT THE SAME TIME inc 1 st at beg of next and every foll 8th row until there are 12 sts, then inc 1 st at beg of every foll 4th until there are 18 sts, then inc 1 st at beg of every alt row until there are 38 sts incorporating all inc sts into double rib and AT THE SAME TIME make a buttonhole every 14th row until 5 buttonholes have been made.
NOTE: Always work bound-off stitches for buttonhole 2 sts in from edge of buttonhole band, adjusting accordingly to accommodate inc sts.
Work even in double rib as set until buttonhole band and collar when slightly stretched reaches center back neck.
Bind off in rib.
Slip stitch button and buttonhole bands and collars in place along Left and Right Front edges, sewing bound-off ends together at center back neck.
Set in the sleeves, matching the center points of the top of the sleeves to the shoulder seams.
Sew side and sleeve seams using mattress stitch.
Sew buttons securely to Left Front button band to correspond with buttonholes on Right Front.

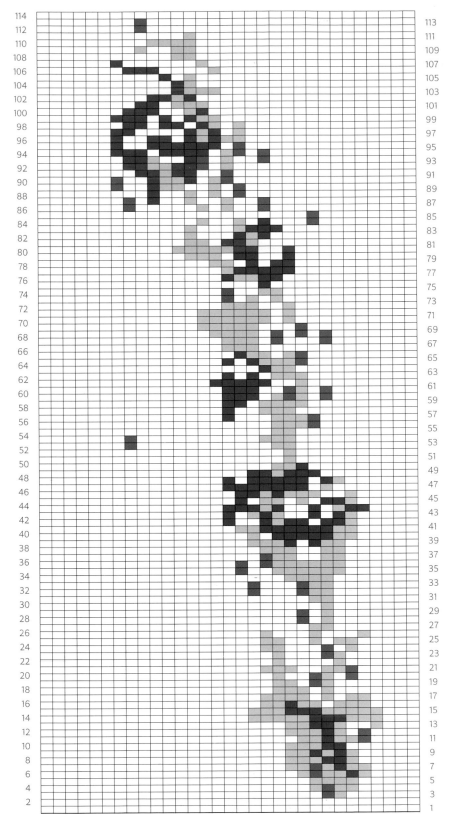

KEY

 MC
knit in MC on a right-side row and
purl in MC on a wrong-side row

WORKED EITHER IN INTARSIA
WHILE KNITTING OR IN DUPLICATE
STITCH ONCE KNITTED

A
knit in A on a right-side row and
purl in A on a wrong-side row or
work in duplicate stitch over MC

B
knit in B on a right-side row and
purl in B on a wrong-side row or
work in duplicate stitch over MC

H
work in duplicate stitch over MC

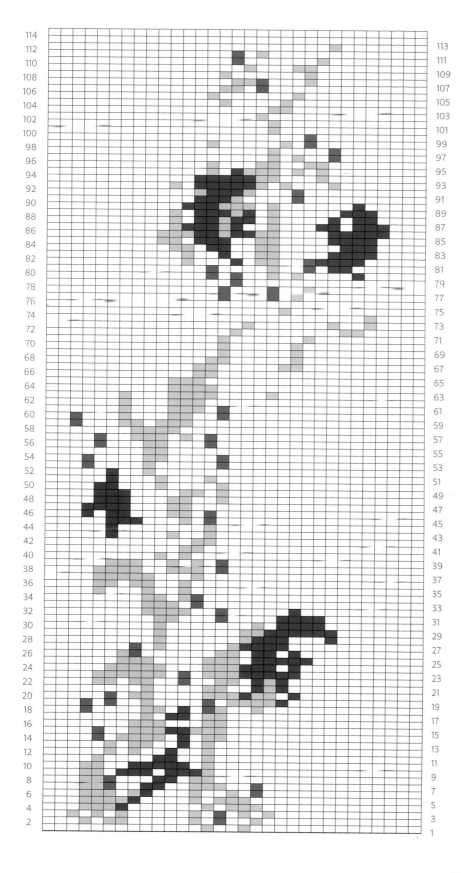

FAIR ISLE BAND SWEATER
WITH SHORT SLEEVES

SIZE

TO FIT BUST	32"	34"	36"	38"	40"
	81cm	86cm	91cm	97cm	102cm
ACTUAL BUST	33"	35"	37"	39"	41"
	82.5cm	87.5cm	92.5cm	97.5cm	102.5cm
LENGTH	20"	20¼"	20½"	21¼"	22¾"
	50.5cm	51cm	51.5cm	54cm	57.5cm
SLEEVE SEAM	4"	4"	4"	4"	4"
	10cm	10cm	10cm	10cm	10cm

YOU WILL NEED

A lightweight wool yarn (3), such as Jamieson's DK,
  in the following colors:
A   6 (6: 7: 8: 8) x ⅞-oz (25g) balls in plum (Plum)
B   5 (5: 6: 7: 7) x ⅞-oz (25g) balls in mustard (Mustard)
Pair each of US sizes 4 and 5 (3.5mm and 3.75mm)
  knitting needles
US size 4 (3.5mm) circular knitting needle

GAUGE

25 sts and 32 rows to 4" (10cm) square measured over
stockinette stitch using size 5 (3.75mm) needles. Adjust
needle size as necessary to obtain correct gauge.

ABBREVIATIONS

See standard abbreviations on page 9.

TO MAKE THE BACK

Using size 4 (3.5mm) needles and A, cast on 99 (105: 111:
117: 123) sts.
ROW 1 (RS): * K1, p1; rep from * to last st, k1.
ROW 2: * P1, k1; rep from * to last st, p1.
The last 2 rows form the single rib (k1, p1 rib) pattern.
Cont to work in single rib as set until Back measures
2" (5cm) from cast-on edge, ending with a WS row.
Change to size 5 (3.75mm) needles.
Beg with a k row, work in St st as set until Back measures
11 (11: 11: 11¾: 12½)"/28 (28: 28: 30: 32)cm from cast-on
edge, ending with a WS row.
Beg with a k row, work 12 rows in St st following chart A
(see page 101), introducing yarn B where required.

FOR 1ST AND 2ND SIZES ONLY
Cont to work in St st in B only for 1" (2.5cm) more,
ending with a WS row.

SHAPE ARMHOLES

FOR 1ST SIZE ONLY
Bind off 4 sts at beg of next 2 rows.
Bind off 2 sts at beg of next 4 rows.
Bind off 1 st at beg of next 2 rows. *81 (–: –: –: –) sts.*

FOR 2ND SIZE ONLY
Bind off 4 sts at beg of next 2 rows.
Bind off 2 sts at beg of next 8 rows. *– (81: –: –: –) sts.*

FOR 3RD SIZE ONLY
Bind off 4 sts at beg of next 2 rows.
Bind off 2 sts at beg of next 10 rows. *– (–: 83: –: –) sts.*

FOR 4TH AND 5TH SIZES ONLY
Bind off 6 sts at beg of next 2 rows.
Bind off 2 sts at beg of next 10 (12) rows. *– (–: –: 85: 87) sts.*
* *

ALL SIZES
Work even in St st until Back measures 20 (20¼: 20½:
21¼: 22¾)"/50.5 (51: 51.5: 54: 57.5)cm from cast-on
edge, ending with a WS row.

WORKING FAIR ISLE COLOR CHANGES

STEP 1 On both knit and purl rows, work as usual to the point of the first color change.

STEP 2 Drop the working yarn and bring the new color yarn over the top of the dropped yarn. Work as usual to the next color change.

STEP 3 Drop the working yarn and bring the new yarn under the dropped yarn. Work to the next color change. Repeat these two steps for all subsequent color changes.

Bind off 7 (7: 8: 8: 8) sts at beg of next 6 (6: 4: 4: 6) rows.
Slip remaining 39 sts onto a stitch holder.

TO MAKE THE FRONT
Work as given for Back to **.
Cont to work in St st until Front measures 17¼ (17¼: 17¼: 18: 19)"/44 (44: 44: 46: 48)cm from cast-on edge, ending with a WS row.

SHAPE FRONT NECK
NEXT ROW (RS): K28 (28: 29: 30: 31), turn, leave rem unworked sts on a stitch holder.
Cont to work in St st on these 28 (28: 29: 30: 31) sts only to create left front of neck but AT THE SAME TIME dec 1 st at neck edge of next 7 alt rows. 21 (21: 22: 23: 24) sts.
Work even in St st until Front measures 20 (20¼: 20½: 21¼: 22¾)"/50.5 (51: 51.5: 54: 57.5)cm from cast-on edge, ending with a WS row.
Bind off 7 (7: 8: 8: 8) sts at beg of next and 2 (2: 1: 1: 2) foll alt rows.

FOR 3RD AND 4TH SIZES ONLY
Bind off – (–: 6: 7: –) sts at beg of next 2 rows.

ALL SIZES
Leave center 25 sts on a stitch holder, rejoin yarn to unworked stitches to work right front of neck and k 1 row. Work to match left front of neck, reversing all shaping.

TO MAKE THE SLEEVES (MAKE TWO)
Using size 4 (3.5mm) needles and A, cast on 67 (71: 75: 79: 83) sts.
Work ½" (1.5cm) in single rib as given for Back, ending with a WS row.
Change to size 5 (3.75m) needles.
Beg with a k row, work 12 rows in St st following chart B, introducing yarn B where required but AT THE SAME TIME inc 1 st at sleeve edges where indicated. 81 (85: 89: 93: 97) sts.

SHAPE TOP OF SLEEVE
Cont to work in St st in B only, bind off 4 (4: 4: 6: 6) sts at beg of next 2 rows and 4 (4: 4: 2: 2) sts on foll 2 rows.
ROW 1 (RS): * K1, skp, k to last 3 sts, k2tog, k1.
ROW 2: P to end of row.
Rep last 2 rows until 29 (31: 33: 35: 37) sts rem.
Bind off 3 sts at beg of next 4 rows.
Bind off rem 17 (19: 21: 23: 25) sts.

TO FINISH

Sew shoulder seams using backstitch.

Using size 4 (3.5mm) circular needle and B, with RS facing and starting at left shoulder seam, pick up and k 31 sts down left front neck, k 25 sts from stitch holder at center front neck, pick up and k 31 sts up right front neck to right shoulder seam, k 39 sts from stitch holder at center back neck. *126 sts.*

Work 6 rounds in single rib as given for Back.

Bind off loosely in rib.

Set in the sleeves and sew side and sleeve seams.

CHART A NOTES
For right-side (knit) rows, read chart from right to left and for wrong-side (purl) rows, read chart from left to right.

CHART A
BACK AND FRONT

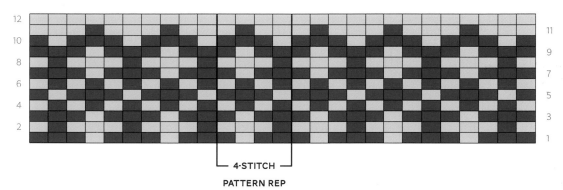

└─ **4-STITCH** ─┘

PATTERN REP

CHART B
SLEEVES

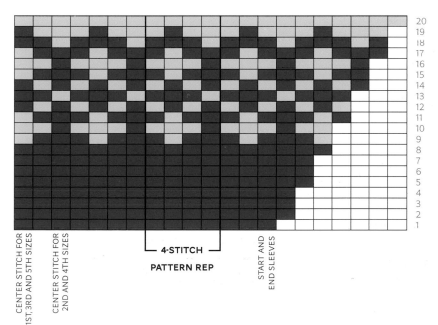

CHART B NOTES
For both right-side (knit) rows and wrong-side (purl) rows, read chart from right to left up to center stitch, work center stitch, then work back from left to right.

└─ **4-STITCH** ─┘

PATTERN REP

CENTER STITCH FOR
1ST, 3RD AND 5TH SIZES

CENTER STITCH FOR
2ND AND 4TH SIZES

START AND
END SLEEVES

TEXTURED CARDIGAN
WITH RIBBED WAIST

SIZE

TO FIT BUST	30" 76cm	32 81cm	34 86cm	36" 91cm	38" 97cm
ACTUAL BUST	31½" 80cm	33½" 85cm	35½" 90cm	37½" 95cm	39¼" 100cm
LENGTH	21" 53.5cm	22" 55.5cm	22½" 57.5cm	23½" 59.5cm	24¼" 61.5cm
SLEEVE SEAM	17" 43cm	17½" 44cm	17¾" 45cm	18" 46cm	18½" 47cm

YOU WILL NEED

10 (11: 12: 13: 14) x 1¾-oz (50g) hanks of a fine-weight yarn (**2**), such as Frog Tree Alpaca Sport Melange, in deep pink (Pumpkin Melange)
Pair each of US sizes 2 and 3 (3mm and 3.25mm) knitting needles
6 (6: 6: 7: 7) small buttons

GAUGE

24.5 sts x 40 rows to 4" (10cm) square measured over stitch pattern using size 3 (3.25mm) needles. Adjust needle size as necessary to obtain correct gauge.

ABBREVIATIONS

sK2po—slip 1 stitch, knit 2 stitches, pass slipped stitch over 2 knit stitches.
See also standard abbreviations on page 9.

PATTERN NOTE

Throughout this cardigan the lace and ridge stitch panel patterns are worked alternately. As the number of stitches are decreased and increased, adjust the pattern panels accordingly to accommodate the lost or gained stitches.

LACE PANEL
(4-ROW REPEAT WORKED OVER 7 STS)
ROW 1 (RS): K1, [yo, sK2po] twice.
ROWS 2 AND 4: Purl.
ROW 3: Work [sK2po, yo] twice, k1.

RIDGE STITCH PANEL
(4-ROW REPEAT WORKED OVER 6 STS)
ROWS 1 AND 3 (RS): K6.
ROW 2: P6.
ROW 4: K6.

TO MAKE A GAUGE SWATCH
Work sample over lace and ridge stitch patterns, as foll:
Using size 3 (3.25mm) needles, cast on 26 sts.
ROW 1 (RS): K3, k1, [yo, sK2po] twice, k6, k1, [yo, sK2po] twice, k3.
ROW 2: P to end of row.
ROW 3: K3, [sK2po, yo] twice, k1, k6, [sK2po, yo] twice, k1, k3.
ROW 4: K3, p7, k6, p7, k3.
Rep last 4 rows until swatch measures 4" (10cm) or larger.

TO MAKE THE BACK
Using size 2 (3mm) needles, cast on 99 (105: 111: 117: 123) sts.
ROW 1: * K1, p1; rep from * to last st, k1.
ROW 2: * K1, p1; rep from * to last st, k1.
The last 2 rows form the seed st pattern.
Cont to work in seed st as set for 10 rows more but AT THE SAME TIME dec 1 st at each end of 7th (7th: 7th: 8th: 8th) row. *97 (103: 109: 115: 121)* sts.
Change to size 3 (3.25mm) needles.
The following 4 rows set the lace and ridge stitch patterns:

FOR 1ST SIZE ONLY
ROW 1 (RS): K6, * k1, [yo, sK2po] twice, k6; rep from * to end of row.
ROW 2: P to end.

ROW 3: K6, * [sK2po, yo] twice, k1, k6; rep from * to end of row.
ROW 4: K6, * p7, k6; rep from * to end of row.

FOR 2ND SIZE ONLY
ROW I (RS): K9, * k1, [yo, sK2po] twice, k6; rep from * to last 3 sts, k3.
ROW 2: P to end.
ROW 3: K9, * [sK2po, yo] twice, k1, k6; rep from * to last 3 sts, k3.
ROW 4: P3, k6, * p7, k6, rep from * to last 3 sts, p3.

FOR 3RD SIZE ONLY
ROW I (RS): K12, * k1, [yo, sK2po] twice, k6; rep from * to last 6 sts, k6.
ROW 2: P to end.
ROW 3: K12, * [sK2po, yo] twice, k1, k6; rep from * to last 6 sts, k6.
ROW 4: P6, k6, * p7, k6; rep from last 6 sts, p6.

FOR 4TH SIZE ONLY
ROW I (RS): K2, * k1, [yo, sK2po] twice, k6; rep from * to last 9 sts, k1, [yo, sK2po] twice, k2.
ROW 2: P to end.
ROW 3: K2, * [sK2po, yo] twice, k1, k6; rep from * to last 9 sts, [sK2po, yo] twice, k1, k2.
ROW 4: K2, * p7, k6; rep from * to last 9 sts, p7, k2.

FOR 5TH SIZE ONLY
ROW I (RS): K5, * k1, [yo, sK2po] twice, k6; rep from * to last 12 sts, k1, [yo, sK2po] twice, k5.
ROW 2: P to end.
ROW 3: K5, * [sK2po, yo] twice, k1, k6; rep from * to last 12 sts, [sK2po, yo] twice, k1, k5.
ROW 4: K5, * p7, k6; rep from * to last 12 sts, p7, k5.

FOR ALL SIZES
The last 4 rows form the lace and ridge stitch patterns. Rep last 4 rows until work measures 6¼ (6½: 6¾: 7: 7¼)"/16.5 (17: 17.5: 18: 18.5)cm, ending with a WS row, but AT THE SAME TIME dec 1 st at each end of next and every foll 6th row until 81 (87: 93: 99: 105) sts rem.

WORK THE RIBBED WAISTBAND
Change to size 2 (3mm) needles.
ROW I: K1, * p1, k1; rep from * to end of row.
ROW 2: P1, * k1, p1; rep from * to end of row.
The last 2 rows form the single rib (k1, p1 rib) pattern.
Cont to work in single rib as set for 18 rows more.
Change to size 3 (3.25mm) needles and beg with Row 1, cont to work 4-row repeat pattern as before, maintaining

placement of each panel as set prior to ribbed waistband, until work measures 5 (5¼: 5½: 5¾: 6)"/13 (13.5: 14: 14.5: 15)cm from top of ribbed waistband, ending with a WS row, but AT THE SAME TIME inc 1 st at each end of every 5th row until there are 99 (105: 111: 117: 123) sts.

SHAPE ARMHOLES
Bind off 3 (4: 4: 4: 5) sts at beg of next 2 rows. *93 (97: 103: 109: 113) sts.*

FOR 1ST, 2ND, AND 3RD SIZES ONLY
Dec 1 st at each end of next 4 rows. *85 (89: 95: –: –) sts.*
Dec 1 st at each end of next 1 (1: 2: –: –) foll 4th (alt: alt: –: –) rows. *83 (87: 91: –: –) sts.*
Dec 1 st at each end of foll 8th (4th: –: –: –) rows. *81 (85: 91: –: –) sts.*

FOR 3RD SIZE ONLY
Dec 1 st at each end of 2 foll 4th rows. *– (–: 87: –: –) sts.*

FOR 4TH AND 5TH SIZES ONLY
Bind off 2 sts at beg of next – (–: –: 6: 6) rows. *– (–: –: 97: 101) sts.*
Dec 1 st at each end of next row. *– (–: –: 95: 99) sts.*
Dec 1 st at each end of foll alt row. *– (–: –: 93: 97) sts.*
Dec 1 st at each end of foll – (–: –: 6th: 4th) row. *– (–: –: 91: 95) sts.*

FOR 5TH SIZE ONLY
Dec 1 st at each end of foll 5th row. *– (–: –: –: 93) sts.*

FOR ALL SIZES
Work even in pattern until armhole measures 7½ (7¾: 8¼: 8¾: 9)"/19 (20: 21: 22: 23)cm, ending with a WS row. *81 (85: 87: 91: 93) sts.*

SHAPE BACK NECK AND SHOULDERS
NEXT ROW (RS): Pattern until there are 26 (28: 29: 31: 32) sts on RH needle, turn and leave rem unworked sts on a stitch holder.
Work each side of the neck separately.
Bind off 3 sts at beg of next row. *23 (25: 26: 28: 29) sts.*
Dec 1 st at beg of foll alt row. *22 (24: 25: 27: 28) sts.*
Bind off 7 (7: 8: 8: 9) sts at beg and dec 1 st at end of next row. *14 (16: 16: 18: 18) sts.*
Dec 1 st at beg of next row. *13 (15: 15: 17: 17) sts.*
Bind off 6 (7: 7: 8: 8) sts at beg and dec 1 st at end of next row. *6 (7: 7: 8: 8) sts.*
Work 1 row.
Bind off rem 6 (7: 7: 8: 8) sts.
With RS facing, rejoin yarn to stitches from stitch holder.

NEXT ROW: Bind off center 29 sts, pattern to end. *26 (28: 29: 31: 32)sts.*
Complete to match first side of neck, reversing all shaping.

TO MAKE LEFT FRONT

Using size 2 (3mm) needles, cast on 54 (57: 60: 63: 66) sts.
ROW I: P – (1: –: 1: –), * k1, p1; rep from * to end of row.
ROW 2: * P1, k1; rep from * to last – (1: –: 1: –) sts, p – (1: –: 1: –).
The last 2 rows form the seed st pattern.
Cont to work in seed st as set for 10 rows more but
AT THE SAME TIME dec 1 st at beg of the 7th (7th: 7th: 8th: 8th) row. *53 (56: 59: 62: 65) sts.*
Change to size 3 (3.25mm) needles.
The following 4 rows form the lace and ridge stitch pattern and 8-st seed stitch button band worked at center front:

FOR 1ST SIZE ONLY

ROW I (RS): K6, * k1, [yo, sK2po] twice, k6; rep from * to last 8 sts, [k1, p1] 4 times.
ROW 2: [P1, k1] 4 times, p to end of row.
ROW 3: K6, * [sK2po, yo] twice, k1, k6; rep from * to last 8 sts, [k1, p1] 4 times.
ROW 4: [P1, k1] 4 times, k6, * p7, k6; rep from * to end of row.

FOR 2ND SIZE ONLY

ROW I (RS): K9, * k1, [yo, sK2po] twice, k6; rep from * to last 8 sts, [k1, p1] 4 times.
ROW 2: [P1, k1] 4 times, p to end of row.
ROW 3: K9, * [sK2po, yo] twice, k1, k6; rep from * to last 8 sts, [k1, p1] 4 times.
ROW 4: [P1, k1] 4 times, k6, * p7, k6; rep from * to last 3 sts, p3.

FOR 3RD SIZE ONLY

ROW I (RS): K12, * k1, [yo, sK2po] twice, k6, rep from * to last 8 sts, [k1, p1] 4 times.
ROW 2: [P1, k1] 4 times, p to end of row.
ROW 3: [SK2po, yo] twice, k6, * [sK2po, yo] twice, k1, k6; rep from * to last 8 sts, [k1, p1] 4 times.
ROW 4: [P1, k1] 4 times, k6, * p7, k6; rep from * to last 6 sts, p6.

FOR 4TH SIZE ONLY

ROW I (RS): K2, * k1, [yo, sK2po] twice, k6; rep from * to last 8 sts, [k1, p1] 4 times.
ROW 2: [P1, k1] 4 times, p to end of row.
ROW 3: K2, * [sK2po, yo] twice, k1, k6; rep from * to last 8 sts, [k1, p1] 4 times.

ROW 4: [p1, k1] 4 times, * k6, p7; rep from * to last 2 sts, k2.

FOR 5TH SIZE ONLY

ROW I (RS): K5, * k1, [yo, sK2po] twice, k6; rep from * to last 8 sts, [k1, p1] 4 times.
ROW 2: [P1, k1] 4 times, p to end of row.
ROW 3: K5, * [sK2po, yo] twice, k1, k6; rep from * to last 8 sts, [k1, p1] 4 times.
ROW 4: [P1, k1] 4 times, * k6, p7; rep from * to last 5 sts, k5.

FOR ALL SIZES

The last 4 rows form the lace and ridge stitch pattern and 8-st seed stitch button band.
Rep last 4 rows until work measures 6¼ (6½: 6¾: 7: 7¼)"/16.5 (17: 17.5: 18: 18.5)cm, ending with a WS row, but AT THE SAME TIME dec 1 st at beg of next and every foll 6th row until 45 (48: 51: 54: 57) sts rem.

WORK THE RIBBED WAISTBAND

Change to size 2 (3mm) needles.
ROW I: K 1 (–: 1: –: 1), * p1, k1; rep from * to end of row.
ROW 2: * P1, k1; rep from * to last 1 (–: 1: –: 1) sts, p 1 (–: 1: –: 1).
These 2 rows form the single rib (k1, p1 rib) pattern.
Cont to work in single rib as set for 18 rows more.
NOTE: Work 8-st button band in single rib instead of seed st over 20 rows of ribbed waistband only.
Change to size 3 (3.25mm) needles.
Beg with Row 1, cont to work 4-row repeat pattern as before, maintaining placement of each panel and seed stitch button band as set prior to working ribbed waistband, until work measures 5 (5¼: 5½: 5¾: 6)"/13 (13.5: 14: 14.5: 15)cm from top of ribbed waistband, ending with a WS row, but AT THE SAME TIME inc 1 st at beg of 5th and at same edge of every foll 5th row until there are 54 (57: 60: 63: 66) sts.

SHAPE ARMHOLE

Bind off 3 (4: 4: 4: 5) sts at beg of next row. *51 (53: 56: 59: 61) sts.*

FOR 1ST, 2ND, AND 3RD SIZES ONLY

Dec 1 st at armhole edge of foll alt row. *50 (52: 55: –: –) sts.*
Dec 1 st at armhole edge of next 3 rows. *47 (49: 52: –: –) sts.*
Dec 1 st at armhole edge of 1 (1: 2: –: –) foll 4th (alt: alt: –: –) rows. *46 (48: 50: –: –) sts.*
Dec 1 st at armhole edge of 1 (1: –: –: –) foll 8th (4th: –: –: –) row. *45 (47: 50: –: –) sts.*

FOR 3RD SIZE ONLY
Dec 1 st at armhole edge of 2 foll 4th rows. – (–: 48: –: –) sts.

FOR 4TH AND 5TH SIZES ONLY
Bind off 2 sts at beg of next and 2 foll alt rows. – (–: –: 53: 55) sts.
Dec 1 st at armhole edge of next row. – (–: –: 52: 54) sts.
Dec 1 st at armhole edge of foll 3rd row. – (–: –: 51: 53) sts.
Dec 1 st at armhole edge of foll – (–: –: 6th: 4th) row. – (–: –: 50: 52) sts.

FOR 5TH SIZE ONLY
Dec 1 st at armhole edge of foll 5th row. – (–: –: –: 51) sts.

FOR ALL SIZES
Cont to work even in pattern until armhole measures 36 rows fewer than the Back to the point where the shaping of the back neck and shoulders begins, ending with a WS row. 45 (47: 48: 50: 51) sts.

SHAPE FRONT NECK
NEXT ROW (RS): Pattern to last 8 sts, turn and leave 8 seed sts on a stitch holder or safety pin.
Bind off 5 sts at beg of next row. 32 (34: 35: 37: 38) sts.
Bind off 2 sts at beg of foll alt row. 30 (32: 33: 35: 36) sts.
Dec 1 st at neck edge of next 4 rows. 26 (28: 29: 31: 32) sts.
Dec 1 st at neck edge of foll 4 alt rows. 22 (24: 25: 27: 28) sts.
Dec 1 st at neck edge of 3 foll 6th rows. 19 (21: 22: 24: 25) sts.
Work 2 rows.

SHAPE SHOULDER
NEXT ROW (RS): Bind off 7 (7: 8: 8: 9) sts, pattern to end of row. 12 (14: 14: 16: 16) sts.
Work 1 row in pattern.
NEXT ROW (RS): Bind off 6 (7: 7: 8: 8) sts, pattern to end of row. 6 (7: 7: 8: 8) sts.
Work 1 row in pattern.
Bind off rem 6 (7: 7: 8: 8) sts.
Mark positions for 6 (6: 6: 7: 7) buttons, placing lowest at center of ribbed waistband, highest at center of neck band (this is added later so you need to estimate its position), and the rest evenly spaced between these two.

TO MAKE RIGHT FRONT
Using size 2 (3mm) needles, cast on 54 (57: 60: 63: 66) sts.
ROW I: * P1, k1; rep from * to last – (1: –: 1: –) sts, p – (1: –: 1: –).
ROW 2: P – (1: –: 1: –), * k1, p1; rep from * to end of row.
The last 2 rows form the seed st pattern.
Cont to work in seed st as set for 10 rows more but AT THE SAME TIME dec 1 st at beg of 7th (7th: 7th: 8th:

8th) row. 53 (56: 59: 62: 65) sts.
Change to size 3 (3.25mm) needles.
Cont to work in pattern reversing as set for Left Front with integral seed stitch button band at center front edge, reversing all shaping but AT THE SAME TIME work buttonholes within seed stitch buttonhole band to correspond with marked button positions as foll:

WORK BUTTONHOLE IN RIBBED WAISTBAND
NEXT ROW (RS): Rib 2 sts, rib2tog, yo, rib 4 sts, pattern to end of row.

WORK BUTTONHOLE IN SEED ST BUTTON BAND
NEXT ROW (RS): Seed st 2, k2tog, yo, seed st 4, pattern to end of row.

TO MAKE THE SLEEVES (MAKE TWO)
Using size 2 (3mm) needles, cast on 37 (39: 39: 41: 43) sts.
ROW I: * K1, p1; rep from * to last st, k1.
ROW 2: * K1, p1; rep from * to last st, k1.
The last 2 rows form the seed st pattern.
Cont to work in seed st as set for 10 rows more but AT THE SAME TIME inc 1 st at each end of every 6th (4th: 4th: 4th: 4th) row. 41 (45: 45: 47: 49) sts.
Change to size 3 (3.25mm) needles.
The following 4 rows set the lace and ridge stitch patterns:

FOR 1ST SIZE ONLY
ROW I (RS): K4, k1, [yo, sK2po] twice, * k6, k1, [yo, sK2po] twice; rep from * to last 4 sts, k4.
ROW 2: P to end of row.
ROW 3: K4, [sK2po, yo] twice, k1, * k6, [sK2po, yo] twice, k1; rep from * to last 4 sts, k4.
ROW 4: K4, p7, * k6, p7; rep from * to last 4 sts, k4.

FOR 2ND AND 3RD SIZES ONLY
ROW I (RS): K6, * k1, [yo, sK2po] twice, k6; rep from * to end of row.
ROW 2: P to end of row.
ROW 3: K6, * [sK2po, yo] twice, k1, k6; rep from * to end of row.
ROW 4: K6, * p7, k6; rep from * to end of row.

FOR 4TH SIZE ONLY
ROW I (RS): K1, k6, * k1, [yo, sK2po] twice, k6; rep from * to last st, k1.
ROW 2: P to end of row.
ROW 3: K1, k6, * [sK2po, yo] twice, k1, k6; rep from * to last st, k1.
ROW 4: P1, k6, * p7, k6; rep from * to last st, p1.

FOR 5TH SIZE ONLY
ROW 1 (RS): K2, k6, * k1, [yo, sK2po] twice, k6; rep from * to last 2 sts, k2.
ROW 2: P to end of row.
ROW 3: K2, k6, * [sK2po, yo] twice, k1, k6; rep from * to last 2 sts, k2.
ROW 4: P2, k6, * p7, k6; rep from * to last 2 sts, p2.

FOR ALL SIZES
The last 4 rows form the lace and ridge stitch patterns. Rep last 4 rows but AT THE SAME TIME inc 1 st at each end of next row and every foll 6th (4th: 4th: 4th: 4th) row until there are 45 (49: 49: 53: 55) sts.

FOR 2ND AND 3RD SIZES ONLY
Work even in pattern for 4 rows.

FOR ALL SIZES
Cont to work in pattern but AT THE SAME TIME inc 1 st at each end of every 6th row until there are 63 (67: 69: 73: 75) sts.
Work even in pattern for 14 (14: 7: 7: 7) rows.
Cont to work in pattern but AT THE SAME TIME inc 1 st at each end of every foll 8th (8th: 7th: 7th: 7th) row until there are 81 (87: 91: 97: 101) sts.
Cont to work even in pattern until Sleeve measures 17 (17½: 17¾: 18: 18½)"/43 (44: 45: 46: 47)cm from cast-on edge.

SHAPE TOP OF SLEEVE
Bind off 3 (4: 4: 4: 5) sts at beg of next 2 rows. *75 (79: 83: 89: 91) sts.*

FOR 1ST SIZE ONLY
Keeping pattern correct, dec 1 st at each end of next 3 alt rows.
Dec 1 st at each end of foll 3rd row, foll 4th row, foll 5th row, foll 4th row, 2 foll 3rd rows, next 9 alt rows, then every row for next 9 rows.

FOR 2ND SIZE ONLY
Keeping pattern correct, dec 1 st at each end of next 3 alt rows.
Dec 1 st at each end of foll 3rd row, 2 foll 4th rows, 5 foll 3rd rows, 9 foll alt rows, then every row for next 9 rows.

FOR 3RD SIZE ONLY
Keeping pattern correct, dec 1 st at each end of next 13 foll 3rd rows, 7 foll alt rows, then every row for next 11 rows.

FOR 4TH SIZE ONLY
Keeping pattern correct, dec 1 st at each end of next 2 rows, then foll alt row, 2 foll 3rd rows, foll alt row, 2 foll 3rd rows, 2 foll alt rows, foll 4th row, foll 5th row, 2 foll 3rd rows, 4

foll alt rows, foll 3rd row, 2 foll alt rows, next row, foll alt row, next row, foll alt row, then every row for next 8 rows.

FOR 5TH SIZE ONLY
Keeping pattern correct, dec 1 st at each end of next row, then foll 3rd row, 3 foll alt rows, 4 foll 3rd rows, 3 foll 4th rows, 3 foll 3rd rows, 7 foll alt rows, next 3 rows, foll alt row, then every row for next 8 rows.

FOR ALL SIZES
Bind off rem 21 (21: 21: 23: 23) sts.

TO FINISH
Sew shoulder seams using backstitch.

WORK NECK BAND
With RS facing and using size 2 (3mm) needles, work seed st across 8 sts on stitch holder at top of buttonhole band on Right Front, then pick up and k 45 (45: 47: 47: 49) sts along Right Front neck, 41 (41: 44: 44: 46) sts along Back neck, and 45 (45: 47: 47: 49) sts along Left Front neck, then work seed st across 8 sts from stitch holder at top of button band on Left Front. 147 *(147: 154: 154: 160)* sts.
Work in seed st for 3 rows.
NEXT ROW (RS): K2, k2tog, yo, work in seed st to end.
Work in seed st for 5 rows.
Bind off in seed stitch.
Set in the sleeves, matching the center points of the top of the sleeves to the shoulder seams.
Sew side and sleeve seams using mattress stitch.
Sew buttons securely to Left Front button band to correspond with buttonholes on Right Front band.

FAIR ISLE AND RIB TANK TOP

SIZE

TO FIT BUST	30"	32"	34"	36"	38"
	76cm	81cm	86cm	91cm	97cm
ACTUAL BUST	31½"	33½"	35½"	37½"	39½"
	80cm	85cm	90cm	95cm	100cm
LENGTH	17"	17¾"	20¼"	20¾"	21"
	43.5cm	45cm	51.5cm	52.5cm	53.5cm

YOU WILL NEED

MC 4 (5: 6: 7: 8) x ⅞-oz (25g) balls of a super fine wool yarn **①**, such as Jamieson's Spindrift, in ecru (Rye)

A super fine yarn **①**, such as Jamieson's Spindrift and Patricia Roberts Fine Cotton in the following colors:

A   1 x ⅞-oz (25g) ball in dark red (Spindrift, Cherry)
B   1 x ⅞-oz (25g) ball in dark green (Spindrift, Pistachio)
C   1 x ⅞-oz (25g) ball in yellow (Spindrift, Daffodil)
D   1 x ⅞-oz (25g) ball in bright pink (Spindrift, Sherbert)
E   1 x ⅞-oz (25g) ball in turquoise (Spindrift, Splash)
F   1 x 1¾-oz (50g) ball in bright green (Fine Cotton, Sap)
G   1 x ⅞-oz (25g) ball in dark blue (Spindrift, Petrol)

Pair each of US sizes 2 and 3 (2.75mm and 3.25mm) knitting needles

GAUGE

30 sts and 32 rows to 4" (10cm) square measured over stockinette stitch using size 3 (3.25mm) needles. Adjust needle size as necessary to obtain correct gauge.

ABBREVIATIONS

See standard abbreviations on page 9.

PATTERN NOTE

Carry the yarn not being worked along the row on the wrong side of the work. Do not carry this yarn too tightly as it will distort the gauge of the knitted piece.

TO MAKE THE BACK

Using size 2 (2.75mm) needles and MC, cast on 113 (121: 129: 137: 145) sts.

ROW 1 (RS): * K1, p1; rep from * to last st, k1.
ROW 2: P1, * k1, p1; rep from * to end of row.
The last 2 rows form the single rib (k1, p1 rib) pattern.
Cont to work in single rib as set for 31 rows more, ending with a RS row.
ROW 1 (INC): Rib 8 (9: 10: 14: 16), inc 1 st, * rib 15 (16: 17: 26: 27), inc 1 st; rep from * to last 8 (9: 10: 14: 16) sts, rib to end. *120 (128: 136: 142: 150) sts.*
Change to size 3 (3.25mm) needles.
ROW 1 (RS): * K2, p2; rep from * to last – (–: –: 2: 2) sts, k – (–: –: 2: 2).
ROW 2: P – (–: –: 2: 2), * k2, p2; rep from * to end of row.
The last 2 rows form the double rib (k2, p2 rib) pattern.
Cont to work in double rib as set until Back measures 9¾ (9¾: 11¾: 11¾: 11¾)"/25 (25: 30: 30: 30)cm from cast-on edge, ending with a WS row.

SHAPE ARMHOLES

Keeping rib correct, bind off 4 sts at beg of next 2 rows.
Dec 1 st at each end of next 7 (8: 11: 11: 13) rows. *98 (104: 106: 112: 116) sts.*
Cont to work even in double rib as set until armhole measures 7¼ (7¾: 8½: 8¾: 9¼)"/18.5 (20: 21.5: 22.5: 23.5)cm, ending with a WS row.

SHAPE SHOULDERS

Bind off 15 (16: 16: 17: 18) sts at beg of next 2 rows.
Bind off 15 (16: 17: 18: 18) sts at beg of next 2 rows.
38 (40: 40: 42: 44) sts.
Change to size 2 (2.75mm) needles.

NEXT ROW (RS): * K1, p1; rep from * to end of row.
The last row forms the single rib (k1, p1 rib) pattern.
Cont to work in single rib as set for 8 rows more, ending with a WS row.
Change to A and cont to work in single rib as set for 1 row more.
Bind off in single rib.

TO MAKE THE FRONT

Using size 2 (2.75mm) needles and MC, cast on 113 (121: 129: 137: 145) sts.
ROW I (RS): * K1, p1; rep from * to last st, k1.
ROW 2: P1, * k1, p1; rep from * to end of row.
The last 2 rows form the single rib (k1, p1 rib) pattern.
Cont to work in single rib as set for 31 rows more, ending with a RS row.
Keeping rib correct, inc 20 sts evenly across the next row. *133 (141: 149: 157: 165) sts.*
Change to size 3 (3.25mm) needles.
Beg with a k row, work in St st following 37-row repeat Fair Isle pattern from charts on pages 112 and 113, starting with Row 1 (1: 17: 17: 17) which is a RS row, until 45 (45: 63: 63: 63) rows have been worked.

DIVIDE FOR NECK SHAPING
NEXT ROW (WS): Pattern 66 (70: 74: 78: 82) sts, place worked sts on a stitch holder, p2tog, pattern to end of row. *66 (70: 74: 78: 82) sts.*

WORK LEFT NECK
Keeping pattern correct, dec 1 st at neck edge on foll 7 (7: 8: 8: 8) 3rd rows.
Work even for 1 (1: –: –: –) rows, ending at side edge.

SHAPE LEFT ARMHOLE
Dec 1 st at neck edge on 13 (14: 14: 15: 16) foll 4th rows but AT THE SAME TIME bind off 4 sts at beg of next row and then dec 1 st at armhole edge on next 9 (10: 12: 13: 14) rows. *33 (35: 36: 38: 40) sts.*
Keeping pattern correct, cont to work even until armhole measures 7¼ (7¾: 8½: 8¾: 9¼)"/18.5 (20: 21.5: 22.5: 23.5)cm, ending with a WS row.

SHAPE LEFT SHOULDER
Bind off 16 (17: 18: 19: 20) sts at beg of next row.
Work even for 1 row.
Bind off rem 17 (18: 18: 19: 20) sts.

WORK RIGHT NECK
With RS facing, rejoin yarn to sts on stitch holder.
Work in pattern to end of row.
Complete to match left neck, reversing all shaping.

TO MAKE THE FRONT NECK BAND

Using size 2 (2.75mm) needles and MC, with RS facing and starting at left front shoulder, pick up and k 54 (58: 62: 66: 68) sts down left front neck edge and 54 (58: 62: 66: 68) sts up right front neck edge. *108 (116: 124: 132: 136) sts.*
ROW I (WS): * K1, p1; rep from * to end of row.
ROW 2 (RS): * K1, p1; rep from * until 52 (56: 60: 64: 66) sts have been worked, sl1, k1, psso, k2tog, * k1, p1; rep from * to end of row.
Keeping rib correct, cont in single rib but AT THE SAME TIME dec 2 sts at center neck as set on foll 3 alt rows. *100 (108: 116: 124: 128) sts.*
Change to A and work 1 row in single rib.
Bind off in single rib.

TO FINISH

Weave in any loose yarn ends on wrong side of work.
NOTE: Lightly spray the finished knitting with water, shape the garment to the correct dimensions and leave to dry flat. Do NOT press the ribbed back.
Sew shoulder and neck band seams using mattress stitch or backstitch.

WORK ARMBANDS
Using size 2 (2.75mm) needles and MC, with RS facing and starting at one side edge, pick up and k 101 (107: 114: 120: 126) sts evenly along armhole edge.
Work 6 rows in single rib.
Change to A and work 1 row in single rib.
Bind off in single rib.
Sew side seams and armband seams using mattress stitch.

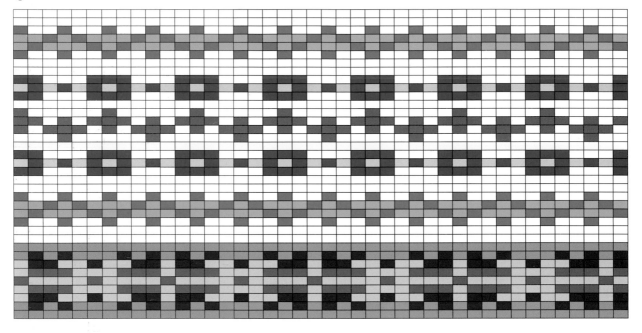

CHART NOTES

For both right-side (knit) rows and wrong-side (purl) rows, starting at marked line on page 113 for size being worked, read chart from right to left and across onto page 112 up to center stitch, work center stitch, then work back from left to right to marked line for size being worked to complete the row.

"FAIR ISLE KNITTING IS A TRADITIONAL WAY to use up scraps of yarn. I really love the thrifty aspect of this technique. You don't actually need a lot of each color, so you can use up small amounts you have left over from other projects to create some lovely, quirky color combinations."

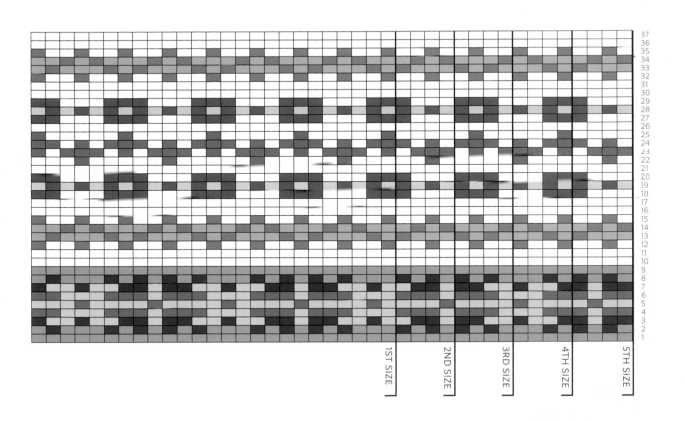

1ST SIZE

2ND SIZE

3RD SIZE

4TH SIZE

5TH SIZE

KEY

☐ **MC** (ECRU)
knit in MC on a right-side row and
purl in MC on a wrong-side row

■ **A** (DARK RED)
knit in A on a right-side row and
purl in A on a wrong-side row

■ **B** (DARK GREEN)
knit in B on a right-side row and
purl in B on a wrong-side row

☐ **C** (YELLOW)
knit in C on a right-side row and
purl in C on a wrong-side row

■ **D** (BRIGHT PINK)
knit in D on a right-side row and
purl in D on a wrong-side row

■ **E** (TURQUOISE)
knit in E on a right-side row and
purl in E on a wrong-side row

☐ **F** (BRIGHT GREEN)
knit in F on a right-side row and
purl in F on a wrong-side row

■ **G** (DARK BLUE)
knit in G on a right-side row and
purl in G on a wrong-side row

CABLED TAM AND SNOOD

....

SIZE
One size, to fit average size woman's head and neck

YOU WILL NEED
A lightweight yarn (3), such as Artesano Alpaca DK, in the following colors:

FOR TAM
2 x 1¾-oz (50g) balls in dark red (Chile)

FOR SNOOD
3 x 1¾-oz (50g) balls in dark red (Chile)

US sizes 3 and 5 (3.25mm and 3.75mm) circular needles, 16" (40cm) long
Set of four US size 3 (3.25mm) double-pointed knitting needles
Cable needle

GAUGE
24 sts and 32 rows to 4" (10cm) square measured over stockinette stitch using size 5 (3.75mm) needles. Adjust needle size as necessary to obtain correct gauge.

"IF YOU ARE PLANNING ON MAKING BOTH these accessories, then I recommend starting with the snood. It is a simple straight tube of knitting so allows you to perfect the cable pattern before moving on to the slightly more complex tam, which is shaped by regularly decreasing stitches over the rounds."

ABBREVIATIONS
C4B cable four back—slip next 2 stitches onto cable needle and hold at back of work, knit next 2 stitches from left-hand needle, knit 2 stitches from cable needle.
C4F cable four front—slip next 2 stitches onto cable needle and hold at front of work, knit next 2 stitches from left-hand needle, knit 2 stitches from cable needle.
make bobble—(k1, p1, k1, p1, k1) into next stitch, turn, p5, turn, pass second, third, fourth and fifth stitches over first stitch, turn, knit into back of first stitch.
s2togkp—slip 2 stitches together, knit 1 stitch, pass 2 slipped stitches over.
T4B cable four back—slip next 2 stitches onto cable needle and hold at back of work, knit next 2 stitches from left-hand needle, purl 2 stitches from cable needle.
T4F twist four front—slip next 2 stitches onto cable needle and hold at front of work, purl next 2 stitches from left-hand needle, knit 2 stitches from cable needle.
See also standard abbreviations on page 9.

40-ROW CABLE PATTERN
ROUND I: * P2, k9, p4, k2, p2, k4, p2, k2, p2; rep from * to end.
ROUND 2: * P2, k9, p4, k2, p2, k4, p2, k2, p2; rep from * to end.
ROUND 3: * P2, C4B, k1, C4F, p4, k2, p2, C4B, p2, k2, p2; rep from * to end.
ROUND 4: * P2, k9, p4, k2, p2, k4, p2, k2, p2; rep from * to end.
ROUND 5: * P2, k4, make bobble, k4, p4, k2, p2, k4, p2, k2, p2; rep from * to end.
ROUND 6: * P2, k9, p4, k2, p2, k4, p2, k2, p2; rep from * to end.
ROUND 7: * P2, k3, make bobble, k1, make bobble, k3, p4, T4F, C4B, T4B, p2; rep from * to end.
ROUND 8: * P2, k9, p6, k8, p4; rep from * to end.
ROUND 9: * p2, k9, p6, T4B, T4F, p4; rep from * to end.
ROUND 10: * P2, k9, p6, k2, p4, k2, p4; rep from * to end.
ROUND II: * P2, C4B, k1, C4F, p4, T4B, p4, T4F, p2; rep from * to end.

ROUND 12: * P2, k9, p4, k2, p8, k2, p2; rep from * to end.
ROUND 13: * P2, k4, make bobble, k4, p4, k2, p8, k2, p2; rep from * to end.
ROUND 14: * P2, k9, p4, k2, p8, k2, p2; rep from * to end.
ROUND 15: * P2, k3, make bobble, k1, make bobble, k3, p4, T4F, p4, T4B, p2; rep from * to end.
ROUND 16: * P2, k9, p6, k2, p4, k2, p4; rep from * to end.
ROUND 17: * P2, k9, p6, T4F, T4B, p4; rep from * to end.
ROUND 18: * P2, k9, p6, k8, p4; rep from * to end.
ROUND 19: * P2, C4B, k1, C4F, p4, T4B, C4B, T4F, p2; rep from * to end.
ROUND 20: * P2, k9, p4, k2, p2, k4, p2, k2, p2; rep from * to end.
ROUND 21: * P2, k4, make bobble, k4, p4, k2, p2, k4, p2, k2, p2; rep from * to end.
ROUND 22: * P2, k9, p4, k2, p2, k4, p2, k2, p2; rep from * to end.
ROUND 23: * P2, k3, make bobble, k1, make bobble, k3, p4, k2, p2, C4B, p2, k2, p2; rep from * to end.
ROUND 24: * p2, k9, p4, k2, p2, k4, p2, k2, p2; rep from * to end.
ROUND 25: * P2, k9, p4, k2, p2, k4, p2, k2, p2; rep from * to end.
ROUND 26: * P2, k9, p4, k2, p2, k4, p2, k2, p2; rep from * to end.
ROUND 27: * P2, C4B, k1, C4F, p4, T4F, C4B, T4B, p2; rep from * to end.
ROUND 28: * P2, k9, p6, k8, p4; rep from * to end.
ROUND 29: * P2, k4, make bobble, k4, p6, T4B, T4F, p4; rep from * to end.
ROUND 30: * P2, k9, p6, k2, p4, k2, p4; rep from * to end.
ROUND 31: * P2, k3, make bobble, k1, make bobble, k3, p4, T4B, p4, T4F, p2; rep from * to end.
ROUND 32: * P2, k9, p4, k2, p8, k2, p2; rep from * to end.
ROUND 33: * P2, k9, p4, k2, p8, k2, p2; rep from * to end.
ROUND 34: * P2, k9, p4, k2, p8, k2, p2; rep from * to end.
ROUND 35: * P2, C4B, k1, C4F, p4, T4F, p4, T4B, p2; rep from * to end.
ROUND 36: * P2, k9, p6, k2, p4, k2, p4; rep from * to end.
ROUND 37: * P2, k4, make bobble, k4, p6, T4F, T4B, p4; rep from * to end.
ROUND 38: * P2, k9, p6, k8, p4; rep from * to end.
ROUND 39: * P2, k3, make bobble, k1, make bobble, k3, p4, T4B, C4B, T4F, p2; rep from * to end.
ROUND 40: * P2, k9, p4, k2, p2, k4, p2, k2, p2; rep from * to end.

TO MAKE THE SNOOD

Using size 3 (3.25mm) circular needle, cast on 174 sts.
Cont to work in the round following cable pattern as foll:

Work rounds 1–10 using size 3 (3.25mm) circular needle.
Work rounds 11–40 using size 5 (3.75mm) circular needle.
Work rounds 1–30 using size 5 (3.75mm) circular needle.
Work rounds 31–40 using size 3 (3.25mm) circular needle.
Bind off loosely in pattern.
Weave in any loose yarn ends on wrong side of work.

TO MAKE THE TAM

Using size 3 (3.25mm) circular needle, cast on 132 sts.
Cont to work in the round as foll:
ROUND 1: * K2, p2; rep from * to end of round.
This last round forms the double rib (k2, p2 rib) pattern.
Cont in double rib as set for 7 rounds more.
NEXT ROUND: K to end of round, inc 71 sts evenly over round by working into front and back of inc sts. *203 sts.*
Change to size 5 (3.75mm) circular needle.
Starting with round 1 of cable patt, work in cable pattern until Tam measures 3½" (9cm) from top of rib.
NEXT ROUND: Cut off yarn and rejoin 23 sts back on previous round—this now the beg of next round. (The central stitch of 9-st bobble cable is now the first stitch.) Divide round into 7 equal sections of 29 sts and place a stitch marker at beg of each section.

SHAPING THE CROWN

Cont to work in cable pattern as set but AT THE SAME TIME adjusting pattern for dec sts and changing to double-pointed needles when there are too few sts to work on circular needle, dec as foll:
ROUND 1: * Pattern 14, s2togkp, pattern 12; rep from * to end.
ROUND 2 AND ALL EVEN-NUMBERED ROUNDS: * Pattern to end.
ROUND 3: * Pattern 13, s2togkp, pattern 11; rep from * to end.
ROUND 5: * Pattern 12, s2togkp, pattern 10; rep from * to end.
ROUND 7: * Pattern 11, s2togkp, pattern 9; rep from * to end.
ROUND 9: * Pattern 10, s2togkp, pattern 8; rep from * to end.
ROUND 11 AND ALL ODD-NUMBERED ROUNDS: Cont to work dec rounds as set working one less stitch either side of double decrease than on previous dec round.
Dec until 21 sts rem.
NEXT ROUND: * S2togkp; rep from * to end of round.
Cut off yarn leaving a long tail. Thread tail through rem sts and secure.
Weave in any loose yarn ends on wrong side of work.

POLKA-DOT SOCKS

SIZE
One size: To fit woman's shoe sizes 7½–9½

YOU WILL NEED
MC 1 x 3½-oz (100g) hank of a super fine wool yarn (1),
 such as Madelinetosh Tosh Sock, in turquoise (Clover)
A   1 x 1¾-oz (50g) hank of a super fine wool yarn (1),
 such as Koigu Premium Merino yarn in coral (Coral)
Set each of five US sizes 1 and 2 (2.25mm and 2.75mm)
 double-pointed knitting needles

GAUGE
26 sts to 4" (10cm) measured over stockinette stitch using
size 2 (2.75mm) needles and MC. Adjust needle size as
necessary to obtain correct gauge.

ABBREVIATIONS
See standard abbreviations on page 9.

> " **YOU CAN KNIT THESE POLKA-DOT SOCKS** in any colorway that you like. As the embroidery is added once the knitting is finished, you can play around with applying different finishing touches with colored yarns in a variety of stitches and patterns. "

TO MAKE THE SOCKS (MAKE TWO)
Using size 1 (2.25mm) double-pointed needles and A,
cast on 78 sts. Arrange sts so there are 22 sts on the first
needle, 17 sts on the second needle, 17 sts on the third
needle, and 22 sts on the fourth needle.
Join in a round and mark beg of round with a stitch marker.
Cut off A and join in MC.
NEXT ROUND: K to end of round.
NEXT ROUND: On first needle, k2, p1, k1, p2, k2, p2, k1,
p1, k2, p1, k1, p2, k1, p1, k2; on second needle, p1, k1, p2,
k1, p1, k2, p1, k1, p2, k2, p2, k1; on third needle, p1, k2,
p1, k1, p2, k1, p1, k2, p1, k1, p2, k1, p1; on fourth needle,
k2, p1, k1, p2, k2, p2, k1, p1, k2, p1, k1, p2, k1, p1, k2.
Repeat last round 11 times more.
Change to size 2 (2.75mm) double-pointed needles.
ROUND 1: On first needle, k2, p1, k1, p2, k2, p2, k1, p1,
k2, p1, k1, p2, k1, p1, k2; on second needle, k17; on third
needle, k17; on fourth needle, k2, p1, k1, p2, k2, p2, k1,
p1, k2, p1, k1, p2, k1, p1, k2.
Repeat last round 4 times more.
ROUND 6 (DEC ROUND): On first needle, k1, ssk, k1, p2,
k2, p2, k1, p1, k2, p1, k1, p2, k1, p1, k2; on second needle
k17; on third needle, k17; on fourth needle, k2, p1, k1, p2,
k2, p2, k1, p1, k2, p1, k1, p2, k1, k2tog, k1.
Cont working as set, working a dec round on the foll 5th,
23rd, 28th, and 48th rounds. *68 sts.*

SHAPE HEEL
NOTE: Cont to work in rows rather than rounds across the
34 sts on first and fourth needles to form heel flap. Hold
other 34 sts on second and third needles for sock upper.
NEXT ROW: On first needle k17, turn.
NEXT ROW: P34, turn.
ROW 1: Sl1, k33, turn.
ROW 2: Sl1, p33, turn.
Repeat last 2 rows 15 times more.
ROW 1: Sl1, k21, ssk, turn.
ROW 2: Sl1, p10, p2tog, turn.
ROW 3: Sl1, k10, ssk, turn.

KNITTING SOCKS IN THE ROUND

"The beauty of knitting in the round with double-pointed needles is that you are always working a right-side row. Most knitters can knit quicker than they can purl so, once you get used to handling the needles, this method is nice and quick."

Distribute the stitches evenly over four needles, then use the fifth empty needle to work the stitches. Mark the beginning and end of
each round with a stitch marker or colored thread.

ROW 4: Sl1, p10, p2tog, turn.
[Rep Rows 3 and 4] 9 times more, until 12 sts rem for heel.
NEXT ROW: K 12 heel sts, pick up and k 17 sts from row ends up first side of heel flap, k 34 sts held on second and third needles for upper, pick up and k 17 sts from row ends of second heel flap and then knit the first 6 heel sts again. *80 sts.*
There are now 23 sts on first needle, 17 sts on second needle, 17 sts on third needle, and 23 sts on fourth needle. Cont working in rounds as foll:
ROUND I: On first needle, k to last 3 sts, k2tog, k1; on second needle, k17; on third needle, k17; on fourth needle, k1, ssk, k to end of round.
ROUND 2: K to end of round.
Repeat last 2 rounds until there are 17 sts on both the 1st and 4th needles. *68 sts.*

SHAPE FOOT
Cont to work in St st until foot measures 7½" (19cm) from back of heel or 2½" (6.5cm) less than required finished foot length.

SHAPE TOE
ROUND I: K to last 3 sts on first needle, k2tog, k2, ssk, k to last 3 sts on third needle, k2tog, k2, ssk, k to end of round.
ROUND 2: K to end of round.
Repeat the last 2 rows until 20 sts rem, ending with a Round 1. *20 sts.*
NEXT ROUND: K 5 sts on first needle, cut off yarn leaving a long tail of approximately 12" (30cm) to sew toe seam.

TO FINISH
Place 10 sts from second and third needles on one needle, then place 10 sts from first and fourth needles on another needle. Using long tail threaded through a yarn needle, graft sets of stitches together as foll:
Hold two needles together, parallel, with needle with long tail at back. Insert yarn needle purlwise into first stitch on front needle and pull yarn through, leaving stitch on knitting needle. Insert yarn needle knitwise into first stitch on back needle and pull yarn through, leaving stitch on knitting needle. Insert yarn needle knitwise into first stitch on front needle and slip stitch off needle. Insert yarn needle purlwise into next stitch on front needle and pull yarn through, leaving stitch on needle. Insert yarn needle purlwise into first stitch on back needle and slip stitch off needle. Repeat until all stitches have been grafted. Weave yarn end into inside of sock. Using A, work large French knots all over sock, but avoiding sole and ribbing.

CABLED CARDIGAN
WITH SHORT SLEEVES

 love

SIZE

TO FIT BUST	32"	34"	36"	38"	40"
	81cm	86cm	91cm	97cm	102cm
ACTUAL BUST	34	36	38"	40"	42"
	86cm	91cm	97cm	102cm	108cm
LENGTH	21"	21½"	22½"	23"	24"
	53cm	55cm	57cm	59cm	61cm
SLEEVE SEAM	6½"	6½"	6½"	6½"	6½"
	16cm	16cm	16cm	16cm	16cm

YOU WILL NEED

MC 5 (5: 6: 6: 7) x 3½-oz (100g) hanks of a lightweight (double-knitting weight) yarn (**3**), such as Juno Fibre Arts Juno Pearl DK, in dusky pink (Savannah)

A 1 x 1¾-oz (50g) ball of a fine-weight yarn (**2**), such as Frog Tree Alpaca Sport, in pink (Rose), for crocheted buttons and edgings (optional)

Pair each of US sizes 3 and 6 (3.25mm and 4mm) knitting needles

Sizes C-2, D-3, and E-4 (2.75mm, 3mm, and 3.5mm) crochet hooks

Cable needle

10 medium-sized buttons

Small amount of polyester stuffing for buttons (optional)

GAUGE

22 sts and 30 rows over 4" (10cm) square measured over stockinette stitch using size 6 (4mm) needles. Adjust needle size as necessary to obtain correct gauge.

ABBREVIATIONS

C2B cable two back—slip 2 sts onto cable needle and leave at back of work, k next st, then k 2 sts from cable needle.

C1F cable one front—slip 1 st onto cable needle and leave at front of work, k next 2 sts, then k 1 st from cable needle.

Cross 2 Left—ignore first stitch, knit into back of second stitch passing behind first stitch, knit into back of first stitch, pass both stitches off the needle together.

Cross 2 Right—ignore first stitch, purl into second stitch passing in front of first stitch, purl into first stitch, drop both stitches off the needle together.

See also standard abbreviations on page 9.

FANCY STRIP PATTERN
(12-ROW REPEAT WORKED OVER 6 STS)

ROWS 1, 3, AND 11 (RS): K6.
ROW 2 AND ALL EVEN-NUMBERED ROWS: P6.
ROW 5, 7, AND 9: C2B, C1F.
ROW 12: Rep row 2.
Repeat Rows 1–12 to form the pattern.

CROSSED STITCH PATTERN
(2-ROW REPEAT WORKED OVER 2 STS)

ROW 1 (RS): Cross 2 Left.
ROW 2: Cross 2 Right.
Repeat Rows 1–2 to form the pattern.

TO MAKE THE BACK

Using size 6 (4mm) needles and MC, cast on 112 (118: 124: 128: 134) sts.
The fancy strip and crossed stitch patts are placed along the row with rev St st at ends of row as foll:
ROWS 1, 3, AND 11 (RS): P 3 (6: 3: 5: 8), k 0 (0: 6: 6: 6), * [Cross 2 Left] 4 times, k6; rep from * 6 times, [Cross 2 Left] 4 times, k 0 (0: 6: 6: 6), p 3 (6: 3: 5: 8).
ROW 2 AND ALL EVEN-NUMBERED ROWS: K 3 (6: 3: 5: 8), p 0 (0: 6: 6: 6), * [Cross 2 Right] 4 times, p6; rep from *

6 times, [Cross 2 Right] 4 times, p 0 (0: 6: 6: 6), k 3 (6: 3: 5: 8).

ROWS 5, 7, AND 9: P 3 (6: 3: 5: 8), [C2B, C1F] 0 (0: 1: 1: 1) times * [Cross 2 Left] 4 times, C2B, C1F; rep from * 6 times, [Cross 2 Left] 4 times, [C2B, C1F] 0 (0: 1: 1: 1) times, p 3 (6: 3: 5: 8).

ROW 12: Rep row 2.

These 12 rows form the fancy strip and four sets of crossed stitch pattern.

Cont to work in pattern as set for 24 (24: 26: 26: 28) rows more.

Change to size 3 (3.25mm) needles.

Cont to work in pattern as set for 22 rows more BUT working 2 rev St st, 2 crossed sts, 2 rev St st for crossed stitch bands.

Change to size 6 (4mm) needles.

Cont to work in pattern as set for 68 (70: 72: 74: 76) rows more BUT working 3 rev St st, 1 crossed st, 3 rev St st for crossed stitch bands.

Cont to work in pattern as set but AT THE SAME TIME bind off 6 (7: 7: 7: 8) sts at beg of next 2 rows, bind off 3 sts at beg of next 4 rows and bind off 2 sts at beg of next 2 (4: 4: 4: 4) rows.

Cont to work in pattern as set but AT THE SAME TIME dec 1 st at beg of next 2 (–: 2: 4: 4) rows. *82 (84: 88: 90: 94) sts.*

Work even in pattern as set for 20 (22: 24: 24: 28) rows, ending with a 12th (4th: 12th: 4th: 12th) row of fancy strip pattern.

FOR 1ST SIZE ONLY

Dec 1 st at beg of next 2 rows. *80 sts.*

FOR ALL SIZES

Bind off 2 sts at beg of next 10 (12: 8: 6: 2) rows, bind off 3 sts at beg of next – (–: 4: 6: 10) rows, bind off 6 sts at beg of next 2 rows, bind off 10 sts at beg of next 2 rows. Bind off rem 28 sts.

TO MAKE THE LEFT FRONT

Using size 6 (4mm) needles and MC, cast on 61 (64: 67: 69: 72) sts.

The fancy strip and crossed stitch patts are placed along the row with rev St st at ends of row as foll:

ROWS 1, 3, AND 11 (RS): P2, * k6, [Cross 2 Left] 4 times; rep from * 4 times, k 0 (0: 6: 6: 6), p 3 (6: 3: 5: 8).

ROW 2 AND ALL EVEN-NUMBERED ROWS: K 3 (6: 3: 5: 8), p 0 (0: 6: 6: 6), * [Cross 2 Right] 4 times, p6; rep from * 3 times, k2.

ROWS 5, 7, AND 9: P2, * C2B, C1F, [Cross 2 Left] four times; rep from * 3 times, [C2B, C1F] 0 (0: 1: 1: 1) times, p 3 (6: 3: 5: 8).

ROW 12: Rep row 2.

These 12 rows set pattern.

Cont to work in pattern as set for 24 (24: 26: 26: 28) rows more.

Change to size 3 (3.25mm) needles.

Cont to work in pattern as set for 22 rows more BUT working 2 rev St st, 2 crossed sts, 2 rev St st for crossed stitch bands.

Change to size 6 (4mm) needles.

Cont to work in pattern as set for 68 (70: 72: 74: 76) rows more BUT working 3 rev St st, 1 crossed st, 3 rev St st for crossed stitch bands.

SHAPE ARMHOLE

Cont to work in pattern as set but AT THE SAME TIME bind off 6 (7: 7: 7: 8) sts at beg of next row, bind off 3 sts at beg of 2 foll alt rows and bind off 2 sts at beg of next 1 (2: 2: 2: 2) alt rows.

Cont to work in pattern as set but AT THE SAME TIME dec 1 st at beg of 1 (–: 1: 2: 2) foll alt rows. *46 (47: 49: 50: 52) sts.*

Work even in pattern as set for 21 (23: 25: 25: 29) rows, ending with a 12th (4th: 12th: 4th: 12th) row of the fancy strip pattern.

FOR 1ST SIZE ONLY

Dec 1 st at beg of next row. *45 sts.*

Work even in pattern for 1 row.

FOR ALL SIZES

Bind off 2 sts at beg of next and 4 (5: 3: 2: –) foll alt rows. Work even in pattern for 1 row.

FOR 3RD, 4TH AND 5TH SIZES ONLY

Bind off 3 sts at beg of next row and – (–: 1: 2: 4) foll alt rows.

Work even in pattern for 1 row.

FOR ALL SIZES

Bind off 6 sts at beg of next row.
Work even in pattern for 1 row.
Bind off 10 sts at beg of next row.
Work even in pattern for 1 row.
Bind off rem sts.

TO MAKE THE RIGHT FRONT

Using size 6 (4mm) needles and MC, cast on 61 (64: 67: 69: 72) sts.

Work as given for Left Front but reversing all shapings and AT THE SAME TIME make a buttonhole over Rows 5 and 6 of the third fancy strip repeat and every foll repeat at center front edge until 11 (11: 12: 12: 12) buttonholes have been worked as foll:

ROW 5 (BUTTONHOLE): Pattern 3 sts, bind off 4 sts in patt, pattern to end.

ROW 6 (BUTTONHOLE): Pattern to sts bound off on previous row, turn, cast on 4 sts, turn, pattern to end of row.

TO MAKE THE SLEEVES (MAKE TWO)

Using size 6 (4mm) needles, cast on 92 (96: 102: 106: 110) sts.

ROW 1: K into back of each st to end of row.
ROW 2: P to end of row.

The fancy strip and crossed stitch patterns are placed along the row with rev St st at ends of row as foll:

ROWS 1, 3, AND 11 (RS): P 7 (9: 12: 14: 16), * [Cross 2 Left] 4 times, k6; rep from * 4 times, [Cross 2 Left] 4 times, p 7 (9: 12: 14: 16).

ROW 2 AND ALL EVEN-NUMBERED ROWS: K 7 (9: 12: 14: 16), * [Cross 2 Right] 4 times, p6; rep from * 4 times, [Cross 2 Right] 4 times, k 7 (9: 12: 14: 16).

ROWS 5, 7, AND 9: P 7 (9: 12: 14: 16), * [Cross 2 Left] 4 times, [C2B, C1F]; rep from * 4 times, [Cross 2 Left] 4 times, p 7 (9: 12: 14: 16).

ROW 12: Rep row 2.

These 12 rows set the pattern.

Cont to work in pattern as set for 24 rows more.

Cont to work in pattern as set for 24 rows more BUT working 2 rev St st, 2 crossed sts, 2 rev St st for crossed stitch bands.

SHAPE TOP OF SLEEVE

Cont to work in pattern as set BUT working 3 rev St st, 1 crossed st, 3 rev St st for crossed stitch bands but AT THE SAME TIME dec 1 st at each end of every row until 28 sts rem.

Work even in pattern for 28 (30: 32: 34: 36) rows.
Bind off rem sts.

TO MAKE THE COLLAR

Using size 6 (4mm) needles and MC, cast on 112 sts.

ROWS 1, 3, AND 11 (RS): P3, * [Cross 2 Left] 4 times, k6; rep from * 6 times, [Cross 2 Left] 4 times, p3.

ROW 2 AND ALL EVEN-NUMBERED ROWS: K3, * [Cross 2 Right] four times, p6; rep from * 6 times, [Cross 2 Right] four times, p3.

ROWS 5, 7, AND 9: P3, * [Cross 2 Left] four times, C2B, C1F; rep from * 6 times, [Cross 2 Left] four times, p3.

ROW 12: Rep row 2.

These 12 rows set the pattern.

Cont to work in pattern as set for 12 rows more BUT working 2 rev St st, 2 crossed sts, 2 rev St st for crossed stitch bands.

Cont to work in pattern as set for 12 rows more BUT working 3 rev St st, 1 crossed st, 3 rev St st for crossed stitch bands.

Bind off.

TO FINISH

NOTE: The top narrow section of the top of the sleeves forms the shoulder.

Sew the side edges of the narrow section at the top of the sleeves to the front and back shoulder, then set in remainder of sleeve.

Sew sleeve and side seams using mattress stitch.

Sew on the collar 1" (2.5cm) in from the front neck edge on both sides to allow the cardigan to button up.

ADD CROCHET EDGING (OPTIONAL)

Using size C-2 (2.75mm) crochet hook and A, work a row of single crochet (sc) up Right Front edge, around Collar edge, and down Left Front edge.

Work a row of sc all the way around the bottom edge of the garment and also around the cast-on edge of the Sleeves.

Using size E-4 (3.5mm) crochet hook and A, work a picot edging into dc rows on Collar, Sleeves, and bottom edge of completed garment as foll:

* Chain 3, 1 sc in next st; rep from * to end.

TO MAKE BUTTONS (OPTIONAL)

Using size D-4 (3mm) crochet hook and A, chain 4 and join with a slip st to first chain to form a ring. Work 8 sc in ring and crochet in rounds increasing 8 dc in each round until you have a disk approximately ¾" (2cm) in diameter. Place a small amount of polyester toy stuffing in center of the crocheted disk, gather the crochet up around the stuffing, and secure.

ADD BUTTONS

Sew buttons securely onto Left Front button band to correspond with buttonholes on Right Front band.

TARTAN SWEATER
WITH THREE-QUARTER-LENGTH SLEEVES

love

SIZE

TO FIT BUST	32" 81cm	34" 86cm	36" 91cm	38" 97cm	40" 102cm
LENGTH	18½" 47cm	19¼" 49cm	20" 51cm	21" 53cm	21½" 55cm
SLEEVE SEAM	13½" 34cm	13¾" 35cm	14" 36cm	14½" 37cm	15" 38cm

YOU WILL NEED

MC 5 (5: 5: 6: 6) x ⅞-oz (25g) balls of a super fine wool yarn (1), such as Jamieson & Smith 2-ply Jumper Weight yarn, in beige (FC45)

Super fine wool yarn (1), such as Jamieson's Spindrift, Rowan Pure Wool 4-ply, and J.C. Rennie Unique Shetland 4-ply, in the following colors:

A 3 (3: 4: 4: 4) x ⅞-oz (25g) balls in gold (Spindrift, Yellow Ochre)

B 2 (2: 2: 2: 2) x ⅞-oz (25g) balls in mid green (Spindrift, Chartreuse)

C 2 (2: 2: 2: 2) x ⅞-oz (25g) balls in brown (Spindrift, Sunrise)

D 1 (1: 1: 1: 1) x ⅞-oz (25g) ball in orange (Spindrift, Amber)

E 1 (2: 2: 2: 2) x ⅞-oz (25g) balls in mid blue (Spindrift, Teviot)

F 1 (1: 1: 1: 1) x ⅞-oz (25g) ball in pale pink (Spindrift, Oyster)

G 1 (1: 1: 1: 1) x ⅞-oz (25g) ball in dark green (Spindrift, Mermaid)

H 1 (2: 2: 2: 2) x ⅞-oz (25g) balls in deep pink (Spindrift, Lipstick)

I 2 (2: 2: 2: 2) x 1¾-oz (50g) balls in light blue (Pure Wool 4-ply, Eau de Nil)

J 1 (1: 1: 1: 1) x 1¾-oz (50g) ball in beige (Unique Shetland 4-ply, Pancake)

Pair each of US sizes 2 and 3 (2.75mm and 3.25mm) knitting needles

GAUGE

22 sts and 44 rows over 4" (10cm) square measured over seed stitch pattern using size 3 (3.25mm) needles and MC. If you need to adjust needle size to attain this gauge, then adjust needles for pattern pieces accordingly.

ABBREVIATIONS

See standard abbreviations on page 9.

PATTERN NOTES

Use the stranding technique for the color pattern, carrying the yarn not in use across the wrong side of the work. If a yarn is carried over several stitches, link it in every 4 stitches. Each row uses no more than two colors. The verticals on the chart on pages 132 and 133 (rectangles with diagonals) are added later in duplicate stitch.

"THE TARTAN PATTERN HERE IS BUILT UP by knitting the Fair Isle sequence and then adding the vertical lines of color in duplicate stitch. These vertical lines can be omitted if preferred, as the initial pattern is interesting in itself. The side gussets add an interest to the shape and mean that, although there are more pieces to knit, none of the tartan pieces are very wide and so are easy to manage."

TO MAKE THE BACK

Using size 3 (3.25mm) needles and A, cast on 133 (141: 149: 157: 165) sts.

Beg with a k row, work in St st following Fair Isle pattern from chart on page 132, starting with Row 1, observing start point for your particular size as marked and bringing in other colors as required and AT THE SAME TIME dec 1 st at each end of every 2nd (3rd: 3rd: 3rd: 3rd) row until there are 107 (119: 127: 135: 143) sts.

Work even in pattern for 27 (22: 24: 25: 27) rows. **

Taking new sts into patt, inc 1 st at each end of every 3rd (4th: 4th: 4th: 4th) row until there are 133 (141: 149: 157: 165) sts.

Work even in pattern until work measures 11 (11½: 11¾: 12¼: 12½)"/28 (29: 30: 31: 32)cm, ending with a WS row.

SHAPE ARMHOLES

Bind off 5 (7: 8: 8: 10) sts at beg next 2 rows.

Dec 1 st at each end of next 4 (3: 5: 8: 7) rows, and then at each end of 1 (2: 2: 1: 2) foll alt row(s), then at each end of foll 3rd (3rd: 5th: 5th: 6th) row, and then on foll 6th (5th: –: –: –) row. *109 (113: 117: 121: 125) sts.*

Work even until armhole measures 7 (7½: 7¾: 8¼: 8¾)"/18 (19: 20: 21: 22)cm, ending with a WS row.

SHAPE BACK NECK AND SHOULDERS

Work until there are 35 (37: 39: 41: 43) sts on RH needle and turn, leaving rem unworked sts on a holder.

Work each side of neck separately.

Bind off 5 sts at beg of next row.

NEXT ROW (RS): Dec 1 st at end of row.

NEXT ROW: Dec 1 st at beg of row.

NEXT ROW (RS): Bind off 8 (9: 9: 10: 11) sts at beg of row and dec 1 st at end.

NEXT ROW: Dec 1 st at beg, work to end of row.

NEXT ROW: Bind off 8 (9: 10: 10: 11) sts, work to end of row.

NEXT ROW: Dec 1 st, work to end of row.

Bind off rem 9 (9: 10: 11: 11) sts.

With RS facing, rejoin yarn to rem sts, bind off center 39 sts, work to end.

Work 1 row then complete to match first side of neck, maintaining pattern and reversing all shaping.

TO MAKE THE FRONT

Work as given for Back to **. *107 (119: 127: 135: 143) sts.*

Now shape sides again, bringing new sts into patt, by inc 1 st at each end of every 3rd (4th: 4th: 4th: 4th) row until there are 121 (131: 143: 153: 163) sts.

Work even for 3 rows (i.e. 1st size has inc on this last row).

DIVIDE FOR NECK

NOTE: The rate of inc of 1 st at each end of every 3rd (4th: 4th: 4th: 4th) row needs to be maintained for a while—so think about when your last inc row was and maintain this pattern. These incs will now only be at side edges.

NEXT ROW (RS FACING, IF NOT, THEN PASS STS TO OTHER NEEDLE): Work until there are 32 (36: 43: 48: 52) sts on RH needle, turn, leaving rem sts on a stitch holder. Work each side of front neck separately.

Cont side-edge shaping as before, as stated, until there are 37 (41: 45: 49: 53) sts.

Work even until work measures 11 (11½: 11¾: 12¼: 12½)"/28 (29: 30: 31: 32)cm and matches Back to this point, ending with a WS row.

SHAPE ARMHOLE

NEXT ROW (RS): Bind off 5 (7: 8: 8: 10) sts, work to end. Work even for 1 row.

Dec 1 st at armhole edge on next 4 (3: 5: 8: 7) rows, 1 (2: 2: 1: 2) foll alt rows, then foll 3rd (3rd: 5th: 5th: 6th) row, and then foll 6th (5th: –: –: –) row. *25 (27: 29: 31: 33) sts.*

Work even in pattern until armhole measures 7½ (7¾: 8¼: 8¾:9)"/19 (20: 21: 22: 23)cm, ending with a WS row.

NEXT ROW: Bind off 8 (9: 9: 10: 11) sts at beg of row. Work 1 row.

NEXT ROW: Bind off 8 (9: 10: 10: 11) sts at beg of row. Work 1 row.

Bind off rem 9 (9: 10: 11: 11) sts.

With RS facing, rejoin yarn to rem sts, bind off 59 sts, work to end.

Complete to match first side of Front, maintaining pattern and reversing all shaping.

TO MAKE THE SIDE PANELS (MAKE TWO)

Using size 3 (3.25mm) needles and A, cast on 57 (67: 71: 75: 79) sts.

Work as given for Back, placing pattern centrally.

Shape sides by dec 1 st at each end of every 4th (6th: 6th: 6th: 6th) row, until 45 (55: 61: 65: 69) sts rem.

Work another 2 (–: 4: 4: 4) rows, ending with Row 26 (36: 34: 34: 34) of pattern.

Cut off yarns.

Change to size 2 (2.75mm) needles and MC only.

Work in single rib (k1, p1 rib), dec evenly in rib as foll:
* K1, p2tog; rep from * to end (working any rem sts at end of row as single rib sts) along first of these rib rows. *30 (37: 41: 44: 46) sts.*

WORKING DUPLICATE STITCH

"Duplicate stitch, which is also known as Swiss darning, is a form of embroidery made to look like knit stitches. Using a tapestry needle threaded with colored yarn, small areas of highlight color can be sewn over the surface of a knitted stitch to add decorative detail without the tricky technique of knitting with multiple colors. When working duplicate stitch, do not pull the embroidered stitches too tight as the fabric will pucker."

STEP 1 Thread a tapestry needle with the highlight color yarn. Bring the needle through from the back to the front of the fabric at the base of the stitch that is to be embroidered over.

STEP 2 Take the tapestry needle, from right to left, under the two loops of the stitch above the one being embroidered over.

STEP 3 Take the needle back through from the front to the back of the fabric at the base of the stitch where it originally came out to complete the duplicate stitch.

STEP 4 If working a horizontal row of duplicate stitches, take the tapestry needle across and bring it through the base of the next stitch to the left and continue as before.

FOR 1ST SIZE ONLY
Rib section is worked without shaping.

FOR 2ND, 3RD, 4TH, AND 5TH SIZES ONLY
Cont to work decs as set of 1 st at each end of every 6th row, even within this rib, until – (33: 35: 38: 40) sts rem and then work even in single rib.

ALL SIZES
Work a total of 32 (26: 28: 28: 30) rib rows, from beg of rib, inc evenly as foll: * k into front and back of knit st, p1; rep from * working any remaining sts as single rib, with an additional inc st if necessary to obtain number of sts required along last rib row. 45 (49: 53: 57: 61) sts.
Cut off MC yarn, change to size 3 (3.25mm) needles and resume pattern on Row 55 (59: 59: 59: 61), ensuring pattern is central. As you work, shape sides by inc 1 st at each end of every 6th (8th: 8th: 8th: 8th) row until there are 57 (67: 71: 75: 79) sts.
Cont until Side Panel measures 11 (11½: 11¾: 12¼: 12½)"/ 28 (29: 30: 31: 32)cm, up to and including last pattern row worked for Back prior to armhole shaping.
Cut off yarns.
Using size 3 (3.25mm) needles and MC only, work from now on in seed st, using the first seed st row to dec sts evenly until 39 (45: 47: 51: 53) sts rem (this means working * k1, p2tog; rep from * for most of this row).
Dec 1 st at each end of foll alt row and then every foll 3rd row until there are 3 sts.
Work even in seed st for 2 rows.
NEXT ROW: Sl1, seed st 1, psso and fasten off.

TO MAKE THE NECK PANELS (MAKE TWO)
Using size 3 (3.25mm) needles and MC, cast on 1 st.
K into front and back of this st to make 2 sts.
Working in seed st, inc at beg of every alt row, until there are 41 sts.
Bind off in seed st.

TO MAKE THE SLEEVES (MAKE TWO)
Using size 2 (2.75mm) needles and MC, cast on 49 (51: 53: 55: 57) sts.
Inc 1 st at each end of every 8th row, work in single rib (k1, p1 rib) for 18 rows.
Change to size 3 (3.25mm) needles.
Work from now on in seed st, maintaining your inc patt, until there are 57 (59: 61: 63: 65) sts.
Work even in seed st for 3 rows, until Sleeve measures 3¼" (8cm).

Inc 1 st at each end of every 14th (13th: 12th: 11th: 10th) row until there are 73 (77: 81: 85: 91) sts.
Work even in seed st until Sleeve measures 13½ (13¾: 14: 14½: 15)"/34 (35: 36: 37: 38)cm, ending with a WS row.

SHAPE TOP OF SLEEVE
Bind off 3 (5: 5: 5: 7) sts at beg of next 2 rows.
Dec 1 st at each end of next 3 (3: 3: 4: 4) rows, foll 2 (2: 5: 5: 7) alt rows, foll 2 (2: 1: 1: –) 3rd row(s), foll 1 (1: 1: 2: –) 4th row(s), foll 4 (4: 7: 7: 9) 5th rows, foll 1 (2: –: –: –) 4th row(s), foll 3 (3: –: 1: 1) 3rd row(s), then foll 3 (4: 4: 1: 2) alt row(s).
Dec 1 st at each end of next 4 (2: 5: 7: 6) rows.
Bind off rem 21 (21: 19: 19: 19) sts in seed st.

TO FINISH
Weave in any loose yarn ends on wrong side.
Lightly press the tartan pattern pieces under a damp cloth. Do not press any seed stitch or rib stitch sections.
Using duplicate stitch (see page 129), embroider the vertical lines over the tartan pattern following the charts on pages 132 and 133. Work the center stitch column in F (pale pink) and then work symmetrically outward in the foll colors: B (mid green), H (deep pink), C (brown), and G (dark green).
If preferred, this additional embroidery may be omitted.
Sew shoulder seams using mattress stitch.
Set in the sleeves, matching the center points of the top of the sleeves to the shoulder seams.
Sew the Side Panels to the Back at each side using mattress stitch, matching tartan patterns.
Sew the remaining Side Panel edges to the Front.
Sew sleeve seams.
Slip stitch Neck Inserts into position, overlapping pieces right over left.
Using H (deep pink), work blanket stitch along the raw edges of the the back neck and down each side of the front neck as far as the Neck Inserts.
If duplicate stitch has been added, using A (gold), embroider a line of cross-stitch along the inside bottom edge of the pattern pieces to prevent curling. Repeat along back neck.
If duplicate stitch has not been added, the fabric may curl at lower edge. To prevent curling, add an edging as foll: Using a size 3 (3.25mm) circular needle and MC, pick up and k 253 (277: 293: 309: 325) sts evenly all around base of garment. Work in seed st for 1¼" (3cm). Bind off in seed st. This adds 1¼" (3cm) to the length given for each size.

CENTER STITCH

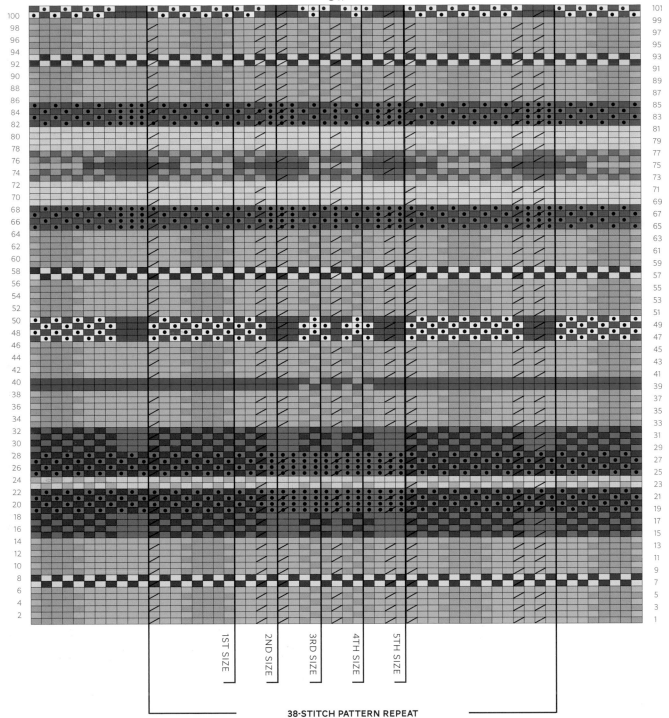

1ST SIZE

2ND SIZE

3RD SIZE

4TH SIZE

5TH SIZE

38-STITCH PATTERN REPEAT

CHART NOTES

For right-side (knit) rows, read chart from right to left, and for wrong-side (purl) rows, read chart from left to right. When starting Row 1, work from line for given size to set position of tartan pattern.

CENTER STITCH

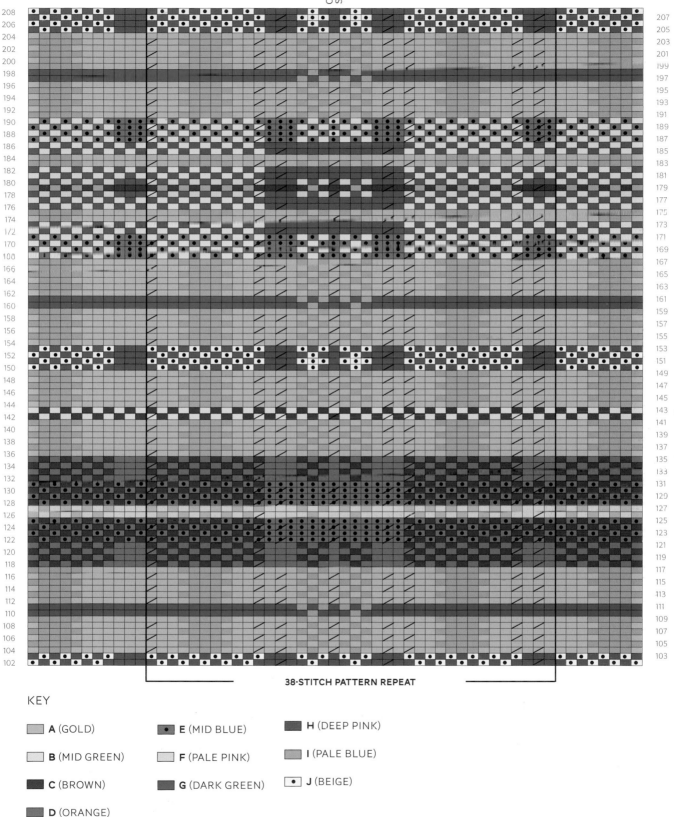

38-STITCH PATTERN REPEAT

KEY

A (GOLD)

B (MID GREEN)

C (BROWN)

D (ORANGE)

E (MID BLUE)

F (PALE PINK)

G (DARK GREEN)

H (DEEP PINK)

I (PALE BLUE)

J (BEIGE)

TARTAN SWEATER **133**

TWEED CAPE

SIZE

	S/M	M/L
TO FIT BUST	32–36"	38–40"
	81–91cm	97–102cm
LOWER EDGE	62"	69"
	157cm	174cm
LENGTH	18"	19"
	45.5cm	49cm

YOU WILL NEED

A 7 (9) x 1¾-oz (50g) hanks of a fine-weight yarn (2),
such as Blue Sky Alpaca Melange, in mustard (Dijon)

B 4 (6) x 3½-oz (100g) hanks of a lightweight (double-
knitting weight) mohair yarn (3), such as Blueberry
Angora Pure Kid Mohair DK, in teal (Teal)

C 1 (1) x 1¾-oz (50g) hank of a fine-weight yarn (2),
such as Blue Sky Alpaca Sport Weight, in bright pink
(Hibiscus) (optional)

Pair of US size 3 (3.25mm) long knitting needles or
US size 3 (3.25mm) circular needle, 32" (80cm) long
1 large button

GAUGE

28 sts and 62 rows to 4" (10cm) square measured over
slip stitch pattern using size 3 (3.25mm) needles. Adjust
needle size as necessary to obtain correct gauge.

ABBREVIATIONS

See standard abbreviations on page 9.

"**THIS CAPE IS
WORKED IN SLIP STITCH,**
which couldn't be easier. You simply
pass the slipped stitch over from the
left-hand needle to the right-hand needle
and carry on knitting as normal. As you
will be working with a large number
of stitches, make sure your straight
needles are long enough or—better
still—use a circular needle with a wire,
but remember you are working in rows
rather than rounds."

SLIP STITCH PATTERN USED THROUGHOUT
(A 12-ROW REPEAT)

NOTE: Slip all slip stitches purlwise. On WS rows move the yarn to the WS when slipping a stitch to avoid strands of yarn across front of work. Row 1 is a RS row.

ROWS 1 AND 2: With A, k1, sl1, k4, sl1, * k2, sl1, k4, sl1; rep from * to last st, k1.

ROWS 3 AND 4: With B, k3, sl2, * k2, sl2; rep from * to last 3 sts, k3.

ROWS 5 AND 6: Rep rows 1 and 2.

ROWS 7 AND 8: With B, k2, sl1, k2, sl1, * k4, sl1, k2, sl1; rep from * to last 2 sts, k2.

ROWS 9 AND 10: With A, k3, sl2, * k2, sl2; rep from * to last 3 sts, k3.

ROWS 11 AND 12: Rep rows 7 and 8.

Repeat Rows 1–12 to form the pattern.

TO MAKE THE CAPE
(KNITTED IN ONE MAIN PIECE)

Using size 3 (3.25mm) needles and B, cast on 392 (416) sts. Work the 12-row repeat slip stitch pattern until work measures 3 (4)"/7.5 (10)cm, ending with a WS row.

MAKE RIGHT ARMHOLE

NEXT ROW (RS): Pattern 46 (54) sts, turn, leave rem unworked sts on a stitch holder.

Work in pattern as set for 9½ (9½)"/24 (24)cm more on these 46 (54) sts only, ending with a WS row.

Place these 46 (54) sts on another stitch holder.

With RS facing, rejoin yarn to 346 (362) sts left on stitch holder and work in pattern to end of row.

MAKE LEFT ARMHOLE

NEXT ROW (WS): Pattern 46 (54) sts, turn, leave rem unworked sts on a stitch holder.

Work in pattern as set for 9½ (9½)"/24 (24)cm more on these 46 (54) sts only to match right side, ending with same pattern row.

Place these 46 (54) sts on another stitch holder.

With WS facing, rejoin yarn to center 300 (308) sts and work in pattern to end of row.

Cont to work as foll:

ROWS 1 AND 2: Pattern to end of row.

ROWS 3, 4, 5, AND 6: Pattern 45 (45) sts, k2tog, pattern to end.

ROWS 7 AND 8: Pattern to end of row.

ROWS 9, 10, 11, AND 12: Pattern 44 (44) sts, k2tog, pattern to end.

Work in pattern but AT THE SAME TIME dec 1 st on every 3rd, 4th, 5th, and 6th rows as set, reducing the number

of sts worked before each dec, until 248 (256) sts rem.

NOTE: Adjust slip pattern as you work to allow for decs.

Work should measure 9½ (9½)"/24 (24)cm to match both sides, ending with the same pattern row. Cut off yarn.

With RS facing, rejoin yarn to sts on stitch holder and work 1 row in pattern across all sts from both stitch holders and central section.

ROW 1: Pattern to end of row. *340 (364) sts.*

ROW 2 AND ALL EVEN-NUMBERED ROWS: Pattern to end of row.

ROW 3: Pattern 66 (66) sts, k2tog, pattern to last 68 (68) sts, k2tog, pattern to end of row.

ROW 5: Pattern 45 (45) sts, k2tog, pattern to last 47 (47) sts, k2tog, pattern to end of row.

ROW 7: Pattern 65 (65) sts, k2tog, pattern to last 67 (67) sts, k2tog, pattern to end of row.

ROW 9: Pattern 44 (44) sts, k2tog, pattern to last 46 (46) sts, k2tog, pattern to end of row.

ROW 11: Pattern 64 (64) sts, k2tog, pattern to last 66 (66) sts, k2tog, pattern to end of row.

ROW 12: Pattern to end of row.

Rep the last 12 rows 3 times more, reducing the number of sts worked before each dec.

ROW 1 (BUTTONHOLE): Pattern 4 sts, bind off 8 sts, pattern to end of row.

ROW 2 (BUTTONHOLE): Pattern to last 4 sts, cast on 8 sts over those bound off in previous row, pattern to end of row. Cont to work Rows 3–12 of 12-row repeat patt, dec as before. *290 (316) sts.*

SHAPE NECK

NEXT ROW (RS): Bind off 24 (24) sts, work until there are 30 (30) sts in pattern on needle, k2tog, pattern to last 56 (56) sts, k2tog, pattern to end of row.

NEXT ROW: Bind off 24 (24) sts, pattern to end of row. *240 (266) sts.*

SHAPE SHOULDERS

ROW 1 (RS): Pattern to end of row.

ROW 2: Pattern 119 (119) sts, k2tog, pattern to end of row. *239 (265) sts.*

ROW 3: K2tog, pattern to last 2 sts, k2tog. *237 (263) sts.*

ROW 4: Pattern 118 (118) sts, k2tog, pattern to end of row. *236 (262) sts.*

ROW 5: Pattern 65 (65) sts, k2tog, pattern to last 67 (67) sts, k2tog, pattern to end of row. *234 (260) sts.*

ROW 6: Pattern 116 (116) sts, k2tog, pattern to end of row. *233 (259) sts.*

ROW 7: K2tog, pattern to last 2 sts, k2tog. *231 (257) sts.*
ROW 8: Pattern 115 (115) sts, k2tog, pattern to end of row. *230 (256) sts.*
ROW 9: Pattern 64 (64) sts, k2tog, pattern to last 66 (66) sts, k2tog, pattern to end of row. *228 (254) sts.*
ROW 10: Pattern 113 (113) sts, k2tog, pattern to end of row. *227 (253) sts.*
ROW 11: K2tog, pattern to last 2 sts, k2tog. *225 (251) sts.*
ROW 12: Pattern 112 (112) sts, k2tog, pattern to end of row. *224 (250) sts.*
ROW 13: Pattern 63 (63) sts, k2tog, pattern to last 65 (65) sts, k2tog, pattern to end of row. *222 (248) sts.*
ROW 14: Pattern 110 (110) sts, k2tog, pattern to end of row. *221 (247) sts.*
ROW 15: K2tog, pattern to last 2 sts, k2tog. *219 (245) sts.*
ROW 16: Pattern 109 (109) sts, k2tog, pattern to end of row. *218 (244) sts.*
ROW 17: Pattern 62 (62) sts, k2tog, pattern to last 64 (64) sts, k2tog, pattern to end of row. *216 (242) sts.*
ROW 18: Pattern 107 (107) sts, k2tog, pattern to end of row. *215 (241) sts.*
ROW 19: K2tog, pattern to last 2 sts, k2tog. *213 (239) sts.*
ROW 20: Pattern 106 (106) sts, k2tog, pattern to end of row. *212 (238) sts.*
ROW 21: Pattern 61 (61) sts, k2tog, pattern to last 63 (63) sts, k2tog, pattern to end of row. *210 (236) sts.*
ROW 22: Pattern 104 (104) sts, k2tog, pattern to end of row. *209 (235) sts.*
ROW 23: K2tog, pattern to last 2 sts, k2tog. *207 (233) sts.*
ROW 24: Pattern 103 (103) sts, k2tog, pattern to end of row. *206 (232) sts.*
ROW 25: Pattern 60 (60) sts, k2tog, pattern to last 62 (62) sts, k2tog, pattern to end of row. *204 (230) sts.*
ROW 26: Pattern 101 (101) sts, k2tog, pattern to end of row. *203 (229) sts.*
ROW 27: K2tog, pattern to last 2 sts, k2tog. *201 (227) sts.*
ROW 28: Pattern 99 (99) sts, k2tog, pattern to end of row. *200 (226) sts.*
ROW 29: Pattern 59 (59) sts, k2tog, pattern to last 61 (61) sts, k2tog, pattern to end of row. *198 (224) sts.*
ROW 30: Pattern to end of row.
ROW 31: K2tog, pattern 79 (75) sts, bind off next 36 (44) sts, pattern to last 2 sts, k2tog.
Work each side separately, beg with left shoulder.
ROW 1 (WS): Pattern 58 (58) sts, k2tog, pattern to end of row.
ROW 2 AND ALL EVEN-NUMBERED ROWS: Pattern to end of row.

ROW 3: K2tog, pattern 55 (55) sts, k2tog, pattern to last 2 sts, k2tog.
ROW 5: Pattern 55 (55) sts, k2tog, pattern to end of row.
ROW 7: K2tog, pattern 52 (52) sts, k2tog, pattern to last 2 sts, k2tog.
ROW 9: Pattern 52 (52) sts, k2tog, pattern to end of row.
ROW 11: K2tog, pattern 49 (49) sts, k2tog, pattern to last 2 sts, k2tog.
ROW 13: Pattern 49 (49) sts, k2tog, pattern to end of row.
ROW 15: K2tog, work 46 (46) sts in patt, k2tog, pattern to last 2 sts, k2tog.
ROW 17: Pattern 46 (46) sts, k2tog, pattern to end of row.
Bind off rem 63 (67) sts. Rejoin yarn to right shoulder and work as given for left side, reversing all shaping.

TO FINISH
Weave in any loose yarn ends on wrong side.
The slip stitch pattern creates a textured fabric that naturally lies flat, so there is no need to press the finished piece.
To round off the otherwise blunt bound-off edges over the shoulders, stitch these seams from the wrong side with backstitch. Start at the neck edge and work toward the shoulder, creating a curved seam for a smooth shoulder line. Finish the seam approximately 1¼–1½" (3–4cm) down from the knitting. Open out the seam on the wrong side and stitch down the seam allowance to create a mini shoulder pad.

WORK COLLAR
With RS facing and starting and finishing 2" (5cm) in from outside edges, pick up and k 120 (120) sts along neck edge using size 3 (3.25mm) needles and B.
ROW 1 (WS): K to end of row.
ROW 2: P to end of row.
ROW 3: K3, M1, k to last 3 sts, M1, k to end.
ROW 4: P to end of row.
Rep last 4 rows once more.
Work even in St st for 4 rows.
Bind off loosely. Turn collar over to RS of work and slip stitch bound-off edge in place to secure.

ADD SURFACE EMBROIDERY (OPTIONAL)
Using C and working in backstitch, embroider additional lines over the surface of the Cape along both vertical columns and horizontal rows of stitches to create a large simple check pattern.

ADD BUTTON
Sew a button securely to Left Front neck edge to correspond with buttonhole on Right Front neck edge.

YARN INFORMATION

It is best to use the yarns specified in the instructions for the designs in this book; they are listed here. If you use a different yarn, compare gauges to ensure the finished results will not differ wildly (see page 8 for how to choose a substitute). The spinner's recommended gauges given here are all measured over stockinette stitch.

ARTESANO ALPACA DK
100% alpaca; 110 yd (100m) per 1¾-oz (50g) ball, 22 sts and 33 rows to 4" (10cm) on US size 6 (4mm) needles
www.artesanoyarns.co.uk

BC-GARN SEMILLA ORGANIC DK
100% organic wool; 175 yd (160m) per 1¾-oz (50g) ball; 22 sts and 33 rows to 4" (10cm) on US size 6 (4mm) needles
www.bcgarn.dk

BLUE SKY ALPACA BULKY
50% alpaca, 50% wool; 41m per 3½-oz (100g) hank; 8 sts to 4" (10cm) on US size 15 (10mm) needles
www.blueskyalpacas.com

BLUE SKY ALPACA MELANGE or SPORT WEIGHT
100% alpaca; 110 yd (100m) per 1¾-oz (50g) hank; 20–24 sts to 4" (10cm) on US sizes 3–5 (3.25–3.75mm) needles
www.blueskyalpacas.com

BLUEBERRY ANGORA PURE KID MOHAIR DK
100% mohair; 240 yd (220m) per 3½-oz (100g) hank; 22 sts and 28 rows to 4" (10cm) on US size 5 (3.75mm) needles
www.blueberryangoras.co.uk

BUFFALO GOLD LUX LACE 2-PLY YARN
45% bison down, 20% silk, 20% cashmere, 15% tencel 328 yd (300m) per 1⅜-oz (40g) hank; gauge is dependent upon project
www.buffalogold.net

DEBBIE BLISS ANGEL
76% mohair, 24% silk; 218 yd (200m) per ⅞-oz (25g) ball; 18–24 sts and 23–24 rows to 4" (10cm) on US sizes 3–8 (3.25–5mm) needles
www.debbieblissonline.com

FROG TREE ALPACA SPORT or SPORT MELANGE
100% alpaca; 128 yd (119m) per 1¾-oz (50g) ball; 24–28 sts to 4" (10cm) on US sizes 3–5 (3.25–3.75mm) needles
www.frogtreeyarns.com

FYBERSPATES SCRUMPTIOUS LACE
45% silk, 55% merino 1,093 yd (1,000m) per 3½-oz (100g) hank; 25–30 sts and 37 rows to 4" (10cm) on US size 3 (3mm) needles
www.fyberspates.co.uk

HABU NON-TWIST COTTON BOUCLÉ LACE
100% cotton; 516 yd (472m) per 1⅝-oz (48g) hank; 36 sts to 4" (10cm) on US sizes 0–2 (2–2.75mm) needles
www.habutextiles.com

HOOPLAYARN
Selvage edges of 100% cotton fabric or cotton-mix jersey; 110 yd (100m) per 17⅝-oz (500g) cone; recommended needle size—US sizes 15–17 (10–12mm)
www.hooplayarn.com

JAMIESON & SMITH 2-PLY JUMPER WEIGHT
100% Shetland wool; 125 yd (115m) per ⅞-oz (25g) ball; 30 sts and 32 rows to 4" (10cm) on US size 3 (3.25mm) needles
www.jamiesonsofshetland.co.uk

JAMIESON'S DK
100% pure new wool; 82 yd (75m) per ⅞-oz (25g) ball; 25 sts and 32 rows to 4" (10cm) on US size 5 (3.75mm) needles
www.jamiesonsofshetland.co.uk

JAMIESON'S SPINDRIFT
100% pure new wool; 114 yd (105m) per ⅞-oz (25g) ball; 30 sts and 32 rows to 4" (10cm) on US size 3 (3.25mm) needles
www.jamiesonsofshetland.co.uk

J.C. RENNIE UNIQUE SHETLAND 4-PLY
100% pure new wool; 235 yd (215m) per 1¾-oz (50g) ball; 28 sts and 36 rows per 4" (10cm) on US size 3 (3.25mm) needles
www.knitrennie.com

JUNO FIBRE ARTS JUNO PEARL (DK)
40% alpaca, 40% merino, 20% silk; 251 yd (230m) per 3½-oz (100g) hank; 22 sts and 29 rows to 4" (10cm) on US size 6 (4mm) needles
www.etsy.com

KOIGU PREMIUM MERINO
100% merino; 175 yd (160m) per 1¾-oz (50g) hank; 28 sts and 36 rows to 4" (10cm) on US size 3 (3mm) needles
www.koigu.com

LAINE ST. PIERRE WOOL
50% wool, 50% polyamide fiber 11 yd (10m) per card of darning wool
www.sajou.fr

MADELINETOSH TOSH SOCK YARN
100% superwash merino wool 395 yd (361m) per 3½-oz (100g) hank; 26–30 sts to 4" (10cm) on US sizes 1–2 (2.5–2.75mm) needles
www.madelinetosh.com

MALABRIGO MERINO WORSTED
100% merino wool; 210 yd (192m) per 3½-oz (100g) hank; 18 sts to 4" (10cm) on US sizes 7–9 (4.5–5.5mm) needles
www.malabrigoyarn.com

NATURAL DYE STUDIO ANGEL LACE 2-PLY
70% alpaca, 20% silk, 10% cashmere; 874 yd (800m) per 3½-oz (100g) hank; recommended needle size—US sizes 000–2 (1.5–2.5mm)
www.thenaturaldyestudio.com

QUINCE & CO. PUFFIN
100% American wool; 112 yd (102m) per 3½-oz (100g) hank; 10–12 sts to 4" (10cm) on US sizes 10¼–13 (6.5–9mm) needles
www.quinceandco.com

PATRICIA ROBERTS FINE COTTON
100% cotton in 1¾-oz (50g) balls; recommended needle size—US sizes 1–2 (2.5–3mm) needles
patriciaroberts.co.uk

ROWAN PURE WOOL 4-PLY
100% superwash wool; 175 yd (160m) per 1¾-oz (50g) ball; 28 sts and 36 rows to 4" (10cm) on US size 3 (3.25mm) needles
www.knitrowan.com

ROWAN PURELIFE BRITISH SHEEPS BREED BOUCLÉ
100% wool; 66 yd (60m) per 3½-oz (100g) ball; 8–9 sts and 13 rows to 4" (10cm) on US size 11 (8mm) needles
www.knitrowan.com

MEET THE TEAM

PUBLISHING DIRECTOR: Jane O'Shea
CREATIVE DIRECTOR: Helen Lewis
COMMISSIONING EDITOR: Lisa Pendreigh
DESIGNER: Claire Peters
PRODUCTION DIRECTOR: Vincent Smith
PRODUCTION CONTROLLER: Aysun Hughes
PATTERN CHECKERS: Marilyn Wilson and Sally Harding
PHOTOGRAPHER: Laura Edwards
PHOTOGRAPHER'S ASSISTANT: Laura Wetherburn
STYLIST: Jazmine Rocks
HAIR AND MAKE-UP ARTIST: Lisa Newson
MODELS: Sam at FM Model Agency, Eva and Rose at
Strike Model Management and Jo Dowbekin,
and also Gavin and Kirk
HAND MODEL: Chinh Hoang

Text, projects, and designs copyright © 2012
Anna Wilkinson

Photography copyright © 2012
Laura Edwards

Artwork, design and layout copyright © 2012
Quadrille Publishing Ltd.

All rights reserved.

Published in the United States by Potter Craft, an imprint of
the Crown Publishing Group, a division of Random House, Inc.,
New York.

www.crownpublishing.com
www.pottercraft.com

POTTER CRAFT and colophon are registered trademarks of
Random House, Inc.

Originally published in the United Kingdom by
Quadrille Publishing Ltd., London, in 2012.

Library of Congress Cataloging-in-Publication Data
Wilkinson, Anna, 1987-
  Learn to knit, love to knit / Anna Wilkinson. -- 1 [edition].
    pages cm
  ISBN 978-0-8041-3680-8 (pbk.) -- ISBN 978-0-8041-3681-5
  (ebook)
1. Knitting--Patterns. I. Title.
  TT825.W554 2013
  746.43'2--dc23

                        2013008139

ISBN 978-0-8041-3680-8
eISBN 978-0-8041-3681-5

Printed in China

Text design by Claire Peters
Photographs by Laura Edwards
Jacket design by Claire Peters
Jacket photographs by Laura Edwards

10 9 8 7 6 5 4 3 2 1

First American Edition

For my parents, Joanna and Martin Wilkinson.

AUTHOR'S ACKNOWLEDGMENTS

I would like to say a very special thank you to my parents, Joanna and Martin, for their continued love, help, and support; and to Richard, thank you for being so understanding and putting up with my untidiness.

I would also like to thank the following people for their brilliant knitting skills and for their help in bringing the designs in this book to life—Joanna Wilkinson, Joan Wilkinson, Leslie Wilkinson, Barbara Booker, Helen Metcalfe, and Lindsay McKean. I am so grateful for all the work you have done and really appreciate the long hours you have put in to help me get everything finished in time. Also, a big thank you to Susanna Samson for being so supportive and encouraging throughout the production of this book.

Lastly, but definitely not least, I want to say a huge thank you to everyone at Quadrille Publishing, in particular Lisa and Claire, and to the fabulous, talented team I have been so lucky to work with on photoshoots. Thank you for not only making this book something that I can be incredibly proud of but also for making this process as enjoyable and fun as possible. Thank you Jazmine and Laura for your energy, creativity, and persistence in making every image in this book so unique and lovely. I am so grateful for all the hard work and enthusiasm that has gone into the making this book.

PUBLISHER'S ACKNOWLEDGMENTS

Thank you to all the owners and staff who allowed us to shoot photographs in the following London locations: Boho Café in Kingston, Collector's Record Centre in Kingston, Flying Cloud Café in Teddington, A French Life in Battersea, Il Molino in Battersea, and The Deli Downstairs in Victoria Park. Thanks also go to the following retailers for their generous loan of clothing: Bertie, Dune, and Tabio.